FOR ALL WHO LOVE
THE BAFFLING,
THE MYSTERIOUS,
THE UNCANNY. . . .

The secrets of the great magicians revealed for
the first time! Find out how much of magic is
simple trickery—how much may be the supernatural powers of stars like The Amazing
Kreskin, Doug Henning, and Uri Geller. Journey
into the world of the unexplained, a world where
mediums talk with the dead and bodies float in
mid-air. From magic in ancient times to the
latest dazzling stunts, it's all here in this sensational, daring expose.

IF YOU'VE EVER BEEN ENTHRALLED BY A
MAGIC SHOW, THIS IS A BOOK FOR YOU!

MASTERS
OF MAGIC

Gene Wright

Illustrations by Rette Kahn

PYRAMID BOOKS 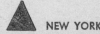 NEW YORK

MASTERS OF MAGIC
A PYRAMID BOOK

Pyramid edition published August 1976

Library of Congress Catalog Card Number: 76-22927

Printed in Canada

Cover picture of Doug Henning in The Magic Show courtesy of
Kenn Duncan Studios.

Pyramid Books are published by Pyramid Publications (Harcourt Brace
Jovanovich, Inc.). Its trademarks, consisting of the word "Pyramid"
and the portrayal of a pyramid, are registered in the United States
Patent Office.

Pyramid Publications (Harcourt Brace Jovanovich, Inc.).
757 Third Avenue, New York, N.Y. 10017

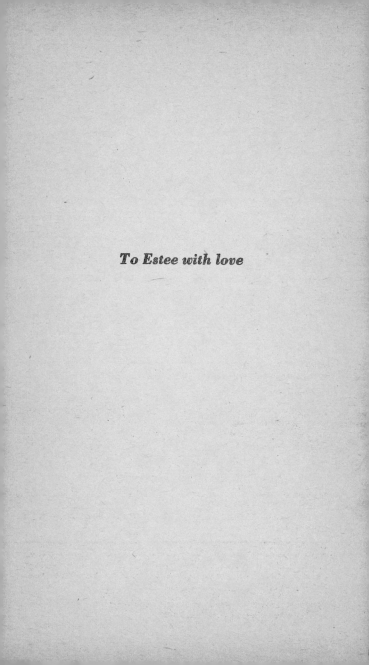

To Estee with love

TABLE OF CONTENTS

1. THE GREATEST MAGICIANS OF ALL TIME   11
2. FAMOUS TRICKS EXPLAINED   33
3. MENTAL MAGIC   61
4. THE UNEXPLAINED: MAGIC AND ESP   79
5. MAGIC ON THE SCREEN   95
6. HOW EASILY CAN YOUR SENSES BE FOOLED?   115
7. ILLUSIONS TO ASTOUND YOUR FRIENDS   123
8. DEVELOPING A SUPER MAGIC MEMORY   141
   GLOSSARY   153

MASTERS
OF MAGIC

Chapter One

THE GREATEST MAGICIANS
OF ALL TIME

How Magic Began

Far back in time, when civilization began to blossom in the parched earth of the Middle East, everyone believed in magic. Scientific knowledge was still in its infancy, and early man thought that the heavens and the earth were controlled by omnipotent gods and goddesses. For plentiful harvests, success in the hunt, and freedom from sickness and war, primitive tribesmen relied on bizarre rituals and strange incantations devised by priests and priestesses who claimed to speak the language of the gods.

The ancient Persians called these divine intermediaries the Magi, and their mysterious working of wonders came to be known as magic. To maintain their positions of great wealth and power, these magician-priests staged awe-inspiring spectacles in the temples where people gathered regularly to offer elaborate fertility rituals and human sacrifices to the gods.

The huddled masses trembled with fear when idols

with the faces of animals and bodies of men and women spoke to them. They stared wide-eyed when a magician materialized in a puff of smoke and heavy temple doors clanged open to indicate that an invisible deity had entered the great halls. The sight of these marvels, set against a backdrop of heavily-incensed altar fires, pillars adorned with mystic symbols and rows of polished black sphinxes, convinced even the most skeptical that the gods were real.

The gods did not exist, of course, and the real magic lay in the magicians' ability to prove they did. So closely guarded were the Magi's secrets that they endured for centuries, until archaeologists rummaging through ruins of forgotten temples of Isis, Baal and Maloch discovered that the solid-looking statues were merely empty shells. It was obvious that magicians stood inside and spoke through openings in lifeless granite lips. Other temples contained sophisticated networks of sound tubes which carried mythical voices to the farthest chamber. And secret panels accounted for a wizard's ability to appear suddenly when a handful of naphtha flashed on an altar fire.

One of the most famous of the early magicians who could perform such wonders was Dedi of De-Snefru. This Egyptian wizard entertained the Pharaoh Cheops who built the Great Pyramid at Gizeh 5,000 years ago. According to the authoritative Westcar Papyrus, an ancient document discovered in 1823, Dedi performed a number of marvels, including the decapitation and restoration of the heads of birds and large animals.

Historians of magic believe that Dedi's secret was a kind of feather-covered mitten with a false head that was placed over the bird's head. After "slicing off" the false head (with an appropriate display of fake blood), Dedi removed the mitten and slipped it into his brightly

12

colored robes. For larger animals such as oxen, Dedi probably used a primitive guillotine with a secret catch that held back the real blade and allowed a concealed, cut-out blade to drop.

Egypt, the so-called "cradle of magic," also claims the oldest magic trick of all, the cups and balls, which is depicted on the wall of a 4,000-year-old burial chamber in Beni Hasan. This venerable sleight of hand has survived dynasties, kingdoms and civilizations, and continues to delight and baffle the spectator.

As the Greek satirist Alciphron wrote in describing a magician of the Second Century A.D. play tricks with tiny white pebbles placed under three overturned dishes. "I do not know how he made them appear together under one. . . . At other times he made them disappear from beneath the dishes and showed them in his mouth. Next . . . he pulled one stone from the nose, another from the ear, and another from the head of the man standing near."

It did not occur to Alciphron that the performer had concealed the pebbles in his hand while pretending to put them under the dishes. The technique of palming (see Chapter 7) enables the magician to produce small objects from any number of unlikely places and has long been a keystone of the art.

Despite their growing popularity in the ancient world, show magicians soon found themselves running for their lives as Christianity gained ascendancy, supplanting the old pagan beliefs. The early fathers of the Church were convinced that magic was the work of the devil, and their inquisitions and witch hunts made no distinction between heretics or witches who were after men's minds and the trickster who wanted only to amuse.

Concerned about the persecution of innocent magicians who faced torture or burning at the stake, Reg-

13

inald Scot, an English magistrate and amateur conjurer, tried to set the world straight by exposing their secrets in a book, *The Discovery of Witchcraft*, published in 1584. Scot's explanation of trickery did little to dispel the fears of righteous fanatics, but proved to be a valuable instruction manual for future conjurers.

By the Eighteenth Century, science had laughed away superstitious beliefs, and magicians, conjurers and wizards became fixtures on street corners and in booths at country fairs. They performed simple effects like the cups and balls, plunged fake knives into their bodies and cut and restored ropes. They were easily identified by aprons equipped with large pockets—the magician's bag of tricks—which held props as well as hid their hands during secret moves.

Many adopted the Merlin-like robes and conical cap of the sorcerer, and they used magic words like "abracadabra," which the ancient Romans believed could cure fever, and "hocus pocus," an invocation of the name of a legendary Italian sorcerer, Ochus Bochus. When the most talented performers, including Fawkes, Gyngell and Pinetti, rented theaters and moved indoors, the magic spectacular was born.

Robert-Houndin and the Golden Age of Magic

Jean Eugene Robert-Houdin (1805-71) would seem an unlikely candidate for his historic role as the "Father of Modern Magic." A slight, meticulously groomed man, he possessed little of the stage presence and personal magnetism of a great performer. Moreover, he did not appear before an audience until he was forty years old, and his career lasted only eight years.

Yet Robert-Houdin swept aside these formidable obstacles, and his magical genius made him the foremost magician of his time. That he made it to the stage at all was a triumph of his strong will and dedication, which overcame the stern prohibitions of his parents while he was growing up in the country town of Blois, France.

At the age of twelve, Robert-Houdin found himself being punished rather than praised for his whimsical mechanical skill. A headmaster had dragged him home by the ear with the complaint that he was distracting his classmates with a miniature gymnasium in which pet mice cavorted on trapezes, slides and a revolving treadmill. After a number of similar incidents, his parents finally threw up their hands in exasperation. Making matters worse, he was soon fired from his job as a lawyer's apprentice for teaching a playful canary in a reception-room cage to pull paper carts and spin discs that produced optical illusions. As a last resort, his parents put him to work in the family business of clockmaking.

Fate seemed to be on his side when by mistake he received a set of volumes on magic instead of the textbooks on clock-making his parents had ordered for him. Before long he had mastered all of the tricks in the book.

Doing tricks for a living was out of the question, however, for his parents equated conjuring with the lowly status of a street sweeper. Instead, Robert-Houdin settled into his job, married and raised a family. But during the next ten years, he discovered a way to combine magic with clock-making in the form of ingeniously constructed wind-up toys. His remarkably lifelife singing birds, tiny dancers pirouetting on tightropes, and miniature conjurers performing the cups and balls were eventually put on display at the Paris Exhibition of 1844. There they caught the eye of French King Louis Philippe, who purchased several, starting a fashion for them.

On the strength of his growing reputation and the demand for magic shows, Robert-Houdin was finally able to raise enough money to lauch his career as a performer. Over the years he had taught himself practically everything there was to know about magic. He had read every book available and studied every performer from street magicians to more established stars such as Phillippe, Comte and Döbler.

The ultimate perfectionist, Robert-Houdin built his own red-and-gold paneled theater with built-in trap-doors and other secret apparatus. He revolutionized magic by designing his stage set to resemble a well-appointed, middle-class living room that seemed above suspicion. Instead of wearing the traditional wizard's robes, he appeared in the formal evening clothes of a gentleman dressed for dinner or a night at the opera.

It was all part of his plan to transform magic into a legitimate performing art, a goal shared by conjurer Jules de Rovère, who had recently coined the elegant word, "prestidigitation," to more accurately describe the grace of his rapid fingerwork. Robert-Houdin's shows would appeal to every member of the family, and he re-solved never to present barbaric feats such as those of the popular Bosco, who wound up his bloody decapitation act by firing a blunderbuss loaded with a canary and catching it on the blade of a sword.

On stage, Robert-Houdin paced his show as a drama, building suspense with each succeeding mystery. His innovative sleights, suspensions and mind-reading effects were so adroitly performed that they baffled even his fellow magicians!

This book is filled with Robert-Houdin's lasting contributions to magic, but one of his most remarkable illusions was performed only once. The occasion was a command performance before King Louis Philippe at his summer palace in St.-Cloud. Robert-Houdin began by borrowing from his noble audience six lace handkerchiefs, which he tied into a bundle and dropped on his magician's table.

Next, he distributed blank cards and asked those present to write down a place to where they would like the handkerchiefs to be conjured. Fanning the collected cards, Robert-Houdin asked the King to select three of them. The first card suggested "beneath a candelabra," which the King thought would be too easy, and the second suggested "the ceiling of the Invalides," site of Napoleon's tomb, which the King thought was too far away. He selected the third suggestion, "a chest beneath the third orange tree on the right of the path of the royal garden."

Covering the handkerchiefs with a frosted glass dome, Robert-Houdin mumbled a few magic words, and when he lifted the dome, the handkerchiefs were transformed into a white turtledove. Louis Philippe immediately sent two servants to his orchard to dig up the orange tree in question while the excited guests watched from a balcony. Sure enough, a small, rusted iron chest was found tangled under the roots and brought inside. The King noted that it was locked. Robert-Houdin lifted the turtledove from its perch on a crystal chandelier and pointed to a key hanging on the bird's neck. The king opened the chest.

Inside the coffer was a parchment scroll bearing the following message; "I, Cagliostro, placed this iron box containing six handkerchiefs among the roots of this orange tree to be found in an act of magic executed on this same day sixty years hence before King Louis Philippe." The monogrammed handkerchiefs were identified by their owners, who joined in the general applause for a magician whose talents were truly magnificent.

How did Robert-Houdin perform such a feat? While his audience was busy filling out the cards, Robert-Houdin's son, Emile, reached out from a hiding place in the backdrop into the hollow tabletop which concealed the bird. He activated a trapdoor and grabbed the handkerchiefs. By the time the King had made a decision, Emile was in the garden planting the box with the original handkerchiefs.

Meanwhile, his father had substituted the collected cards for a similar set in his coat pocket. The trick deck contained repetitions of the same three suggestions, each in a different handwriting. Believing he was making a free choice, Louis Philippe selected one of the carefully-grouped series of three which Robert-Houdin had practically thrust into the monarch's hands. (The technique, a card sharper's specialty known as forcing, involves guiding the victim's attention to the object you want him to choose and making him take it before he can reconsider.) The rest was a calculated gamble that the King would select the spot most convenient to the occasion.

His dream fulfilled and his fortune made, Robert-Houdin retired to his lavish estate in St. Gervais near Blois and wrote his invaluable books on magic. He spent his declining years transforming his house into a magic chateau with secret rooms, descending floors and electric clocks.

Following in Robert-Houdin's footsteps was Alexander Herrmann (1843-96), a German by birth but an

American by adoption, and the youngest and most famous member of a family of conjurers. Herrmann created the enduring stereotype of a show magician by affecting a dapper mustache and goatee that added a mysterious, Faustian touch to his charming, low-key personality.

His specialty was the throwaway trick. Introducing himself to the audience, Herrmann would casually remove his white kid gloves and pause while looking for a place to put them. Seemingly as an afterthought he would toss them into the air and the gloves instantly vanished. Later in the evening, he would repeat this amazing feat by unexpectedly causing a canary and birdcage to disappear from his right hand.

How he accomplished this trick was ingenious. Looped around Herrmann's left wrist was a thin strip of strong cloth which extended across his back to the opposite sleeve, where it emerged with a tiny hook. The gloves and birdcage were fitted with eyelets which caught onto the hook and shot up his right sleeve when he thrust out his left hand to wave a wand. The effortless perfection of Herrmann's performance belied the great skill and sense of timing necessary to achieve it.

Although his theatrical engagements earned him millions and enabled him to travel in his own yacht and private railroad car, Herrmann delighted in giving free, impromptu performances. Porters were amazed to find tips coming from their ears and noses, and waiters looked perplexed when he tossed glasses and bottles into the air and made them disappear. President U.S. Grant became one of his victims when Herrmann plucked cigars from Grant's long gray whiskers during a White House gala.

Meanwhile, across the Atlantic in England, J.N. Maskelyne (1839-1917) and his partner, David Devant, added innovations and new illusions to the magician's traditional bag of tricks that made these performers the most imitated prestidigitators in the world.

Maskelyne and Devant probably vanished more people than were ever reported to the missing persons bureaus. Herrmann featured disappearances also, but the British magicians brought the illusion to perfection as the famous "Mascot Moth." A beautiful girl in a gossamer costume fitted with moth's wings danced around a huge candle until she came too close to the flame. Suddenly she shriveled away—in full view of the audience!

The method of the vanish was ingenious. The girl's dress was constructed of thin metal bracings that held its shape even when empty. She joined the wings over her face and was lowered through a trapdoor while a camouflaged tube rose slightly through the floor behind her.

The dress stayed in place until Devant gave the signal for a stagehand to yank the dress through the tube by means of a cord the girl had secretly dropped inside it. *Pouff,* the moth girl was gone.

Magic is also indebted to Maskelyne and company for what is perhaps the most famous illusion of all— "The Floating Lady." A beautiful female assistant rose majestically from the stage in the Egyptian Hall, Maskelyne's "home of mystery," and a hoop was passed around her reclining body to prove that nothing but magic held her floating in space.

Going himself one better, Maskelyne later floated himself. At one moment he was addressing the audience, and the next, while continuing to talk, he was rising into the air over their bewildered heads. A spotlight followed his rise to the theater's dome, where he turned around and gently floated back down.

Few knew Maskelyne was also one of those watching

the startling effect. It was a dummy fitted with a mask molded from his face—complete with brush mustache —that was lifted into the air via thin wires darkened with lampblack. The substitution was made during a quick lighting change, and Maskelyne's talent for ventriloquism gave a voice to the suspended dummy.

Maskelyne's American counterpart was Harry Kellar (1849-1922), who modeled his show after the Englishman's and even named his Philadelphia theater the Egyptian Hall. A balding, round-faced man with an impish grin and twinkling eyes, Kellar looked like a clean-shaven Santa Claus. Magic historian Walter Gibson believes that Kellar was the inspiration for Frank Baum's *The Wizard of Oz*, which was written at the height of Kellar's fame and incorporated many of his amiable "humbug" mannerisms.

Barely educated, afflicted with a speech impediment, his fingers thick and stubby, Kellar probably had more personal faults to overcome than any other magician. He nevertheless rose to the top of his profession, and although never superlative at sleight of hand, he conquered all with his personality and meticulous attention to detail.

When variety shows, called vaudeville—which featured singers, dancers, acrobats, jugglers and just about anyone with a talent to amuse—captured the public's fancy in the Nineteenth Century, the Golden Age of Magic was at last at hand. Polished conjurers like Kellar became star attractions in new theaters throughout America, and performers like Thurston and Raymond filled the bottom of the bill while they learned their craft.

Kellar and Herrmann, vying for the title of "Monarch of Magic," livened up the scene with their bitter, ten-year battle for the best theater bookings. When they played the same towns, Herrmann would hire men to paste his posters over Kellar's. Kellar would retaliate, followed by Herrmann again, until the posters were five or six layers deep. Once, Kellar appeared at a Herrmann show and walked up to the stage when a volunteer was requested. Enraged, Herrmann began to reveal Kellar's secrets during his performance and his rival quickly followed suit.

Another famous magician of the time was Billy Robinson (1861-1918), a former assistant of Herrmann and Kellar, who was known as "Chung Ling Soo." He adopted a Chinese identity in imitation of Ching Ling Foo, a Chinese conjurer who had brought oriental magic to the West. Dressed in an embroidered robe, Ching Ling Foo would waddle onto the stage, wave a long silk scarf and produce a 100-pound fish bowl filled with live goldfish. Looking at the scarf as if it might contain something else, Ching waved it again and produced a smiling Chinese boy. The bowl had been concealed under the robe, and the boy hung from his back. As you might guess, it was difficult to walk naturally strapped with a harness containing a huge weight—a secret Ching successfully hid by never walking anywhere without his strange, shuffling gait.

Although Robinson did not go to the uncomfortable lengths of Ching Ling Foo, he kept up the masquerade by speaking with a Chinese accent, eating only Chinese food, and forcing his wife Dorothy to adopt the identity of "Suee Seen." Robinson's greatest illusion was his sensational "Bullet-Catching Trick," which climaxed in his catching on a silver tray two bullets fired directly at him.

The trick had been promoted as a "death-defying stunt," and one fateful night in London during World War One, Robinson proved that the words were no idle boast. As usual, his wife went into the audience with two bullets which volunteers marked with a knife and dropped into a cup she carried. Later, the caught bullets would be identified by the volunteers as proof they had indeed been fired.

On stage the bullets were loaded with gunpowder and wadding and rammed home into antique rifles. Actually, Robinson's wife had already handed the original bullets to him with the tray, after handing to the riflemen a similarly marked pair hidden inside her cup.

The trick rifles cracked and blazed on cue, but this time something went wrong. Instead of his standard response of reeling back and smiling, Robinson lurched forward with a look of panic on his face. The bullets and tray clattered to the floor as he fell dead with a bullet through his heart.

An inquest revealed that the old muskets had been plugged with steel to keep the round bullet from being discharged by the firing pin. Over the years, a screw that held one of the plugs in place had corroded and loosened, thus allowing gunpowder to leak through, and the bullet had fired. It was the magicians' ultimate nightmare and a horrifying pun—the trick that backfires.

Houdini: The Man Behind the Legend

A short, powerfully-built man with curly hair, hypnotic eyes, a commanding voice and a mysterious, charismatic presence, Harry Houdini (1874-1926) was so dazzling a showman that his name still shines above the others as a universal symbol of magic. The stories of his miraculous escapes from burglar-proof safes, padlocked milk cans and packing cases nailed shut and thrown into icy rivers are legendary.

Many people old enough to have witnessed Houdini's electric performance still believe that he possessed a supernatural gift that enabled him to dematerialize his body and escape from any enclosure. Others claim that Houdini could shrink the bones in his arms and legs and slip from knotted ropes and locked handcuffs.

The truth was less arcane but equally astonishing. His secret was a fanatical devotion to body control which began when he was growing up as Erich Weiss in Appleton, Wisconsin. Forced to compete with tall, strapping farm boys for odd jobs he needed to help support his Hungarian immigrant family, Houdini built up his scrawny frame with rigorous exercises that led him continually to challenge his physical limits. In his autobiography he described several of the agonizing disciplines he forced upon himself, one of which, accomplished at the age of nine, was to pick up pins with his eyelashes while hanging upside down.

His impoverished parents counted their blessing when Houdini was apprenticed to a locksmith, a steady trade that would ensure his future. But in spite of showing an unusual aptitude for the job, he hated the regular hours and dull routine and, as he later punned, "I soon made a bolt for the door."

At twelve Houdini escaped to a job with a circus that was passing through Appleton, and he began his unusual education. From back-breaking labor as a roustabout who put up the tents, he learned how to tie secure knots and slip them free in an instant. From sideshow magicians he learned the tricks of the trade. From "rubbermen" contortionists he discovered how to stretch his well-muscled body and nudge his shoulders out of joint without hurting himself, a skill later useful for escaping from straitjackets.

When a friend gave him a copy of *The Memoirs of Robert-Houdin,* he decided at once that his destiny was to be a magician. He changed his name to Houdini to honor "my guide and my hero," adding an "i" to the French conjurer's name to mean *like Houdin,* and, for the sake of alliteration, crowning it with Harry.

Hiring his younger brother Theo as his assistant, the 17-year-old "Great Houdini" made his debut in a Manhattan beer hall with an act that featured a speeded-up version of an illusion borrowed from J. N. Maskelyne. Tying Theo into a large bag, Houdini padlocked him inside a trunk and sat on top while a screen was drawn. A moment later Theo was sitting on the trunk and Houdini was locked inside. Under cover of the screen, Houdini had pushed open a secret panel in the lid while Theo hurriedly pulled out a thick thread that basted the bottom of the bag. Once they had exchanged places, Houdini had ample time to re-stitch the thread while his brother fumbled with the lock.

Eventually the effect would become another of Houdini's bafflers, but at that time audiences and vaudeville booking agents were unimpressed. Houdini married during this difficult period, and he and his wife, Bess, spent the next few years playing penny arcades and sideshows. When bookings were slim, they traveled with a patent medicine show that used magic as a come-on for the "doctor" who peddled a miracle cure that was actually sarsaparilla-flavored grain alcohol.

Houdini was playing a third-rate variety house in Chicago when he gambled on a publicity stunt to introduce his own brand of magic. He hoped a dramatic boast would finally put his name in lights. "I can escape from any set of handcuffs or cell in this city," Houdini announced to the few bored reporters who turned up backstage. The warden of the municipal jail swallowed the bait, and a few days later Houdini was manacled and locked up.

While the reporters joked about the foolhardy challenger, Houdini walked into the warden's office and tossed the handcuffs in front of them. To counter criticism that he had somehow managed to steal the keys and conceal them, Houdini did it again, this time after being stripped and searched. The story of a naked man breaking out of jail made sensational headlines.

Not many people knew that Houdini had never forgotten his early expertise with locks. He had visited the jail the night before, not only to introduce himself, but to identify the type of lock he would have to open. The handcuffs presented no problem, for they merely had to be struck against a hard surface at the proper angle to spring open. For the cell door, Houdini used a small lock pick of his own invention, which he was able to conceal while nude.

During the search, Houdini passed the pick from hand to hand and put it into his bushy hair while his hands were being inspected. When his hands and hair were being simultaneously inspected by suspicious spectators, Houdini would hide the narrow object in his throat and later regurgitate it, a trick taught to him by an old Japanese sword swallower. When a cell lock was too far away to reach, Houdini would manipulate the pick with his toes, which were almost as nimble as his fingers.

Within five years Houdini had earned the title, "The World's Foremost Escape King," after breaking out of top-security jails in the United States, Canada, England, France, Germany and Russia. His exploits garnered more newspaper space than those of kings and presidents. To keep up the constant flow of publicity that brought long lines to the box office. Houdini accepted escape-proof containers from all challengers.

Safes were relatively easy since they were designed to thwart burglars breaking into them, not magicians *breaking out* of them, a fact that did not occur to the enraptured public. Packing crates and coffins were carefully doctored by Houdini's staff while they transported them to the theater in a covered truck. Two-inch screws were substituted for the secure six-inch size so that Houdini could hammer them out with his hands while the band played loud marching music to mask the noise. When a volunteer from the audience tied him up, Houdini would expand his chest and arm muscles to obtain enough slack to work with later. If the knots were too tight, Houdini would resort to a razor blade concealed in his lapel.

In his famous "Water Torture Cell" escape, Houdini's feet were locked into a wooden stock, and he was plunged head first into a glass tank filled with water. A screen was pulled down over the tank. When the screen was removed seconds later, Houdini stood dripping wet in front of the tank. The stock was still tightly locked. Few suspected it had false rivets which Houdini had opened after grabbing metal glass supports and working his body up and out of the water. The trick sounds deceptively simple, but it required such physical dexterity that hardly anyone could figure out how it was done.

Illusions were never enough for Houdini. He seemed compelled to prove time and again that he was a superman by staging dangerous outdoor stunts. He wriggled out of straitjackets while hanging from flagpoles of tall buildings, endured being buried alive to prove that it was all a matter of breath control, and happily dropped into rivers while handcuffed and locked in boxes.

In a sense Houdini was a victim of his own legend. The end finally came not from a death-defying stunt, but as a result of a banal accident. A McGill University student, visiting him backstage in Montreal, asked Houdini if it were true that he could sustain any blow to the midsection without injury. Houdini nodded idly and continued going through his mail when the young man's fist suddenly shot out and hammered away four times. Caught unawares, the fifty-two-year-old Houdini had not braced his stomach muscles, and he staggered over to a couch. Dismissing the numbing pain as a torn muscle, the aging superman went on to play an engagement in Detroit where he developed an uncontrollable fever and collapsed onstage. His appendix had ruptured, peritonitis had set in and it was too late to save him. Houdini died on Halloween afternoon in 1926—a day that is remembered in his honor as National Magic Day.

The Decline
and Rebirth of Magic

With Houdini gone, Howard Thurston (1869-1936) became the world's premier prestidigitator. Like Houdini, Thurston was a teen-age runaway who had earned his magician's wand in the boondocks where tough audiences often pelted an inept performer with rotten vegetables.

After a brief career as a juvenile delinquent and

race-track tout, Thurston attended and graduated from divinity school. On his way to the University of Pennsylvania Medical School, where he hoped to become a missionary doctor to atone for his past sins, Thurston made another abrupt about face and became a magician. Changing trains in Albany en route to the university, he spotted a poster announcing that Herrmann was playing in town. Lured by the spell his boyhood idol had cast when he saw him perform in his home town of Columbus, Ohio during the 1876 Centennial celebration, Thurston never got back on the train.

Thurston's specialty was coin palming. He became so adept at it that once, during a show at an Indian reservation, an elderly Indian demanded the silver coins he pretended to pluck from the old man's clothing. A chief who witnessed a repeat performance agreed that no trickery was apparent, and Thurston was out $20.

In 1908 Thurston purchased Kellar's show and added new effects to present one of the grandest stage spectacles of all. He vanished dozens of automobiles with people in them, and pianos while people played them. He also devised an ingenious version of the Indian rope trick (see Chapter 2) and shot women from cannons. His apparatus was so large that he needed ten railway baggage cars to accommodate it during his many worldwide tours. In addition, he replaced uniformed male assistants with pretty girls, adding to his magic shows a touch of sex appeal.

Ironically, at the same time that magic was reaching its greatest heights in the 1920s, the number of theaters for magic was shrinking. Vaudeville houses were being turned into movie theaters to satisfy the public demand for this fascinating new illusion of movement and speech. To make matters worse, many theater-goers were staying at home to listen to the new marvel of radio.

With a few notable exceptions—the Great Raymond, Dante and Blackstone, who played nightclubs and shared the bill with movies—big magic went into a steep decline. Until television came to the rescue, big magic almost faded as popular entertainment. But a generation that had grown up never having seen a magician was soon captivated by the world of fantasy that TV magicians Harry Blackstone, Jr., Melbourne Christopher, Mark Wilson and The Great Randi brought into their living rooms.

One of those watching at home in Winnipeg, Canada, was six-year-old Doug Henning, who would one day restore magic to its former glory. "I started training myself to become a magician after I saw a levitation act on the Ed Sullivan Show," Henning recalls. At fourteen Henning was good enough to command five dollars per appearance at birthday parties and scout meetings, and he later graduated to coffee-houses and rock festivals. He used his earnings to buy more magic books and effects.

After earning a degree in psychology from McMaster University, Henning convinced the Canadian Arts Council to give him a $4,000 grant to study magic full time. The result was a show put together in Toronto, called *Spellbound*. Two enterprising producers who realized that magic was staging a big comeback brought him to New York and built Broadway's *The Magic Show* around him.

Walking onto the stage in a T-shirt and satin jeans, the pencil-slim Henning flashed a winning, buck-toothed smile, brushed his long hair from his eyes and nervously performed his first illusion. The loud applause told Henning that the old mysteries had not lost their appeal, and for the first time in thirty-five years, a successful magic show was back on Broadway.

"I don't look like a magician and that adds an element of surprise," twenty-eight-year-old Henning explains. "But my illusions are all updated versions of tricks handed down from generation to generation, things that Houdini, Blackstone and Thurston did."

Today's magicians are enjoying an unprecedented popularity, and performers like Kreskin, card wizard Derek Dingle, Mark Wilson and Uri Geller, who may or may not be a magician (see Chapter 4), are show-business headliners.

As The Great Randi points out, the revival of magic "is a sign that our society is still healthy. When people stop being enthralled by a magician who can make a lady vanish, it will mean that the world has lost its most precious possession: its sense of wonder."

Chapter Two

FAMOUS TRICKS EXPLAINED

The great stage illusions represent the ultimate evolution of the art of magic. Here is conjuring on a grand scale, where a human being can defy gravity and float in the air, where a carload of people can vanish in a puff of smoke, and where a beautiful girl can be transformed into a tiger—all with the simple wave of a magic wand.

In magic jargon, such conjurers who perform with large props and complicated apparatus are called "illusionists," and their magic requires the facilities of a stage equipped with trapdoors, "flying" wires and moving platforms.

Assistants are also required, most of whom are not seen, for they work behind the scenes manipulating equipment and following the magician's cues. To ensure secrecy, magicians employ their own stagehands who are required to sign oaths that stipulate they will never reveal the workings of an illusion.

Women are now the magician's traditional onstage assistants, and their traditional victims. In the name of entertainment, illusionists have shot women from cannons, skewered them with swords, sliced off their heads and sawed them in half. Some women's liberation groups may construe these simulated tortures as symbolic acts of masculine domination, but the magician has a more practical purpose in mind. A pretty girl in a revealing costume provides a highly effective misdirection to take the audience's attention from the conjurer's secret moves.

An illusionist is more than merely a performer of outsized tricks, however. He is also an accomplished actor who knows how to build suspense and mystery. Moreover, every great illusionist, from Professor Pinetti to Doug Henning, has possessed that indefinable something known as "star quality."

Most of the great illusions that follow are still being performed today. Hopefully, knowing how they are done will add to your enjoyment of the magician's performance.

The Indian Rope Trick

A turbaned street magician (*jadoo*) attracts a crowd from people passing along the road. He throws one end of a long rope into the air and it stays there, slowly rising until it has completely uncoiled and stretches toward the heavens, rigid and unsupported. The *jadoo* orders a small boy to climb the rope, but he refuses. Threatened by the magician's stick, the boy reluctantly shimmies up and shouts down insults even after he has vanished from the top of the rope.

Enraged, the magician clenches a large dagger in his teeth and climbs up after him. At the top of the rope there is a violent struggle punctuated by the boy's bloodcurdling shrieks. Now it is the crowd's turn to scream as a bloody arm hurtles to the ground, followed by another, two legs and, finally, the boy's head.

The magician slides back down, wiping the bloody blade on his robes, and the rope falls to the ground. Hastily he gathers the severed pieces into a wicker basket and closes the top. Muttering an incantation, the magician gives the basket a kick and, wonder of wonders, out pops the smiling boy!

If you think that the legendary Indian Rope Trick is an impossibility, there are many magicians who agree with you. Jasper and John Nevil Maseklyne, Thurston and Houdini, among others, offered thousands of dollars to anyone who could perform the fabled effect for them, but the money was never collected. Most doubt that the trick was ever performed, although the reliable Moslem historian, Ibn Batuta, swore that he saw it in India during the Fourteenth Century. One theory holds that witnesses were hypnotized by the *jadoo* into believing they saw the rope trick.

A more plausible explanation was offered by Harry Price in his book, *Confessions of a Ghost Hunter,* and by the Great Raymond, who claimed he saw a faked version in Calcutta in 1912. According to Price, the trick was most likely performed in bright sunlight on a narrow street or between two trees. When the magician threw the rope into the air, tiny grappling hooks, concealed at the end, connected with a sloping wire his accomplices had strung between two buildings or trees. The wire was then drawn taut, causing the rope to appear to rise. Clouds of incense burning at the rope's base rose to the top, which was placed directly in line with the sun. Spectators looking up saw only a dazzling cloud and believed that the boy had disappeared.

To create the illusion of the boy's death, pieces of a

freshly slaughtered and shaved monkey (concealed in the jadoo's voluminous robes) were dropped. The falling limbs directed the audience's eyes away from the magician, and gave the boy a chance to slip into a leather harness inside the magician's robes and thus be transported unseen when the magician returned to the ground. Accomplices cut the supporting wire and the rope collapsed. When the basket was opened the boy, emerging secretly from the magician robes, dropped inside, hidden from view by the lid.

Modern illusionists produce less gruesome stage versions of this trick in which it isn't necessary to slaughter an innocent monkey, but the mystery of the original legend persists. Perhaps, as magician Will Dexter claims, "There is an Indian Rope Trick, yes. But *the* Indian Rope Trick, no."

The Robot Chess Champion

Studying the chessboard over the top of his half-glasses, Benjamin Franklin leaned back and smiled, confident that his last move had escaped the trap set for him. His opponent's eyes clicked mechanically as a wooden arm reached out and clawed a white bishop and dropped it opposite Franklin's king. Nodding three times, the creature gave its mute signal of checkmate.

The Parisian audience applauded wildly, delighted to have witnessed the defeat of the renowned American ambassador to France, who joined the list of champions and royalty outwitted by the chess-playing robot.

Automatons were the greatest magic attraction of

the day, and ingenious craftsmen, including Robert-Houdin, filled the demand by creating doll-like figures that duplicated human motion. Jacques de Vaucanson, for instance, drew crowds with his clockwork duck that was almost natural enough to fool another duck, and which was unpleasantly close to nature. "When corn was thrown before it," recalled Sir David Brewster, a nineteenth-century historian of magic, "the duck stretched its neck to pick it up, swallowed it, digested it, and discharged it in a digested condition."

Imitative movement was one thing, but a machine able to think out complicated chess moves was another, and it was the Robot Chess Champion that captured the public's attention all over the world. It became an international pastime either to beat the robot or to figure out how it worked.

Invented in 1769 by Wolfgang von Kempelen, a Hungarian nobleman, the chess player was constructed in the image of a mysterious Turkish pasha and became known simply as the "Turk." The figure was smaller than life-size, seemingly ruling out the possibility that a man was hidden inside it. The cabinet behind which it was seated, however, was obviously large enough to hold a man doubled over. To prove there was no one inside, von Kempelen always began a performance by opening the cabinet doors one by one and holding a candle on the other side. The audience saw only the gears, cylinders and levers that supposedly made the Turk move.

After being wound up with a large key, the Turk began the match, removing the pieces he captured himself and nodding his head to signal an attack or a checkmate.

When the Turk came to the United States in 1836,

Edgar Allan Poe was among the defeated challengers. But noticing that one of the exhibitor's assistants always disappeared during the chess match, Poe put two and two together and concluded that the man hid inside the cabinet watching the game through the figure's chest and moving his arms up through the Turk's to play.

Poe was on the right track, but the secret did not come to light until the robot was auctioned off to a chess club in Philadelphia after its owner's death. It was more complicated and ingenious than anyone had imagined.

A man *was* hidden inside the cabinet, and he slid from one side to another on a seat that rode along hidden tracks as the doors were opened. His back rested against a moveable panel and his legs were hidden under a black cloth that, from a distance, passed for the floor.

The sound of the key being wound was the signal to begin, and the concealed chess player pulled down from a wall a chessboard with two holes in each square, something like today's portable chessboards. One set of holes was for chess pieces so the concealed player could keep track of the game, and the other was for the tip of a metal rod connected to the robot's playing arm. When the rod was lifted, the robot's arm rose and was guided to the square corresponding to the concealed player's chessboard. Slipping the rod into the proper hole, the man gave it a twist to the right to open the hand and a twist to the left to close it around the piece above.

The challenger's moves could be seen from under the Turk's board, where dangling metal disks were drawn up by magnetized pieces. Movement of the puppet's head and eyes was accomplished by similar rods.

The Floating Lady

"Rise" the magician commands his comely young assistant who lies on a couch in a deep hypnotic trance. For a moment nothing happens, and the audience grows tense. The magician repeats the command with a few more mesmeric passes of his hands and, finally, the unconscious girl obeys. Instead of rising to her feet, however, she floats up to the magician horizontally until her rigid body is well over his head.

"She lies asleep in space," the magician intones, "suspended by nothing but the power of thought."

There seems to be no trickery involved. How could there be? The girl is floating in the center of the stage, well away from backdrops and props. As further proof that there are no hidden supports, the magician passes a large steel hoop over the girl from end to end, not once but *twice*, from each direction. The hoop is passed down to front-row spectators who ascertain that it is solid.

A moment later the smiling girl is back on the ground wide awake, her gravity restored. Although you probably don't notice it, the girl walks off the stage rather awkwardly. Under her pretty dress is an uncomfortable steel brace that runs from shoulder to knee. While two male assistants were placing her on the couch, they were also locking the brace into an s-shaped rod permanently connected to a bar parallel to the girl's body. (See illustration.)

The "float" is accomplished by means of four nearly

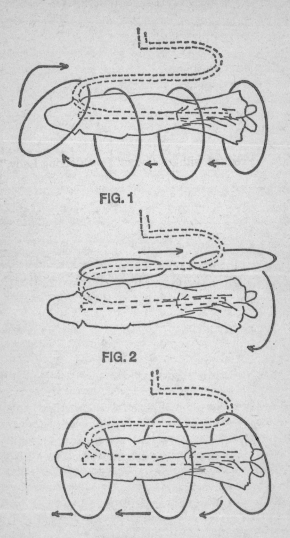

FIG. 1

FIG. 2

FIG. 3

invisible, black-painted wires that run from the parallel bar up into the flies to weights and counterbalances backstage. Hooking her free foot over the braced one, the girl makes sure that the hanging folds of her costume conceal the underside of the mechanism. The ingenious design of the gooseneck rod makes it possible for the magician to seem to pass the hoop completely around her body.

The great John Nevil Maskelyne, of whom we spoke earlier, is credited with inventing "The Floating Lady," which Kellar later updated in his "The Levitation of Princess Karnac." In Kellar's version, the girl was covered with a sheet and then made to vanish in mid-air, an effect made possible by a wire frame—complete to the tips of the girl's shoes—sewn into the cloth. The assistant tumbled off the couch into a trapdoor while the cover was being thrown over her. The frame simply collapsed when it was yanked off the gooseneck rod, which was simultaneously drawn into the flies.

Magicians call this illusion a levitation. Although levitations are mentioned in the Bible and the Koran, it wasn't until Robert-Houdin came along that a conjurer was able to duplicate these miracles. Robert-Houdin began his demonstration by asking his eight-year-old son Eugène to stand on a stool set on a plank supported by two carpenter's horses at either end. Eugène's elbows rested on canes placed on two more stools. Sniffing a bottle of ether that his father held under his nose, the boy fainted, his head sagged and his feet left the stool he was standing on.

One by one the magician removed the stool, the cane and the stool to his left, but Eugène stayed in the air. With his little finger, Robert-Houdin lifted his son's feet until his body was horizontal, and he seemed to be

41

floating on his right elbow. As further proof of the boy's weightlessness, the magician took away one of the horses. Now the plank, the remaining stool, the cane and the boy *all* seemed to float.

Many believed that the ether anesthetic was the key to the mystery, and some even complained to authorities that Robert-Houdin was sacrificing his son's health "for the pleasures of the public." The secret was far more complicated, of course, and ether had nothing to do with it. The unmistakable odor was wafted from backstage and was nowhere near Eugène, who became weightless thanks to an iron body brace that locked into iron rods concealed in the cane, stool, plank, horse and stage. The change of angle was made possible by a pivot gear under the boy's armpit.

Nowadays magicians use more portable equipment such as belts with hooks that engage with a harness worn by assistants. If the lighting is right, a sheet of glass can be used. Another modern method is to crank up the girl through the stage floor by means of a rod hidden inside the magician's trouser leg.

It's All Done with Mirrors

The first magicians to realize the possibilities of mirrors were probably the priests of ancient Egypt and Babylon. With the help of drawings and concave mirrors, they were able to "prove" their divinity by projecting faces of the gods through smokey altar fires and onto temple walls. Medieval magicians like Cagliostro used a similar technique to conjure up demons, as did spirit mediums later to summon visages of the dearly departed.

Perhaps that is the reason ghosts, mummies, corpses and decapitated heads came to be the subjects of mirror illusions. Stage magicians expanded the repertoire when they discovered that the reflective properties of mirrors could be used to *vanish* as well as to produce and to change one image into another. John Henry Pepper, an English chemistry professor, is credited with inventing the first mirror illusion, "Pepper's Ghost," in 1863.

In this illusion, a ghost seems to rise from the floor of the stage. The actor runs it through again and again with his sword until the cackling spirit disappears in a flash of light. The illusion depends on a huge, tilted sheet of plate glass and an assistant hidden in a black-velvet-lined orchestra pit that is well below the audience's sight level. The image of the ghost is merely his reflection on the plate glass. The phantom disappears as stage lights are brought up, and the bottom light is turned off. The effect is similar to seeing yourself in a shop window.

Of the many new effects made possible by mirrors, none was more chilling than the illusion of "The Blue Room."

The stage is dressed as a dusty crypt festooned with glistening cobwebs and bathed in an eerie blue light. A volunteer from the audience grins nervously as the magician fits him into an upright coffin, then leaves the stage. A church bell tolls ominously. Two hooded monks suddenly appear and begin to chant a mournful dirge: "Ashes to ashes, dust to dust, all you living will soon be thus."

Wait a minute! What is happening?

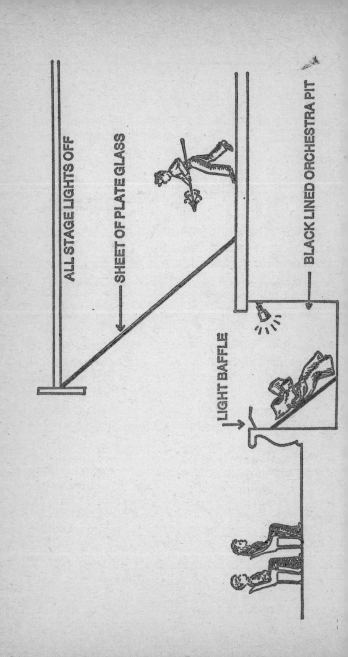

ALL STAGE LIGHTS OFF

SHEET OF PLATE GLASS

BLACK LINED ORCHESTRA PIT

LIGHT BAFFLE

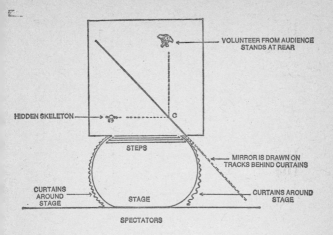

VOLUNTEER FROM AUDIENCE STANDS AT REAR

HIDDEN SKELETON

STEPS

MIRROR IS DRAWN ON TRACKS BEHIND CURTAINS

CURTAINS AROUND STAGE

STAGE

CURTAINS AROUND STAGE

SPECTATORS

The volunteer's eyes are fading into dark sockets, his nose is becoming a large cavity. Within a few minutes his clothing and flesh have decayed completely until there is nothing left of him but a skeleton. The *memento mori* is chilling, and the audience is relieved when the process is reversed and the man reappears in the coffin —still alive. The applause, however, indicates delight at having been horrified, which is why people flocked to the Tavern of the Annihilation in Paris to see this macaber version of the famous "Blue Room" illusion.

A great tourist attraction during the 1930s and 1940s, the Tavern in the Montmarte district featured tables that were inverted coffins and waiters dressed as undertakers. "May I recommend our aperitif of grave worms," a waiter would offer in sepulchral tones. "Or perhaps you would prefer a deadly microbe. We have them all on tap. Please name your poison." Whatever the customer ordered, he always received a tepid beer served in a skull-shaped tankard.

Based on an effect of John Henry Pepper and another magician, Thomas W. Tobin, the illusion derived its name from the blue light that was used to conceal a partially silvered mirror. As such a mirror has a bluish cast, it was almost impossible for the audience to see it.

"The Blue Room" could change a man into a woman, bring a statue to life or make any number of startling transformations. The secret was simple. The mirror was slowly slid out from behind the scenery at the side of the stage. It simultaneously blocked the object or person to be vanished and reflected the object or person to be conjured.

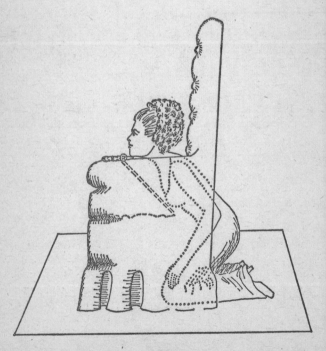

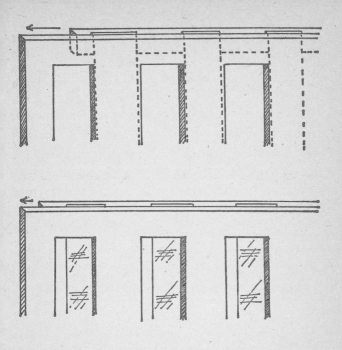

A volunteer from the audience stands at point A, and the partially silvered mirror is slowly pushed forward until the hidden skeleton at point B is reflected at point C, slowly replacing the audience's view of the man.

In "The Decapitated Princess", another mirror illusion, a disembodied head of a living girl rests on the blade of a sword. She tells the audience how it felt to have had her head cut off! As the illustration below shows, the girl is actually kneeling behind a mirror which reflects the seat cushion making it appear as the seat back.

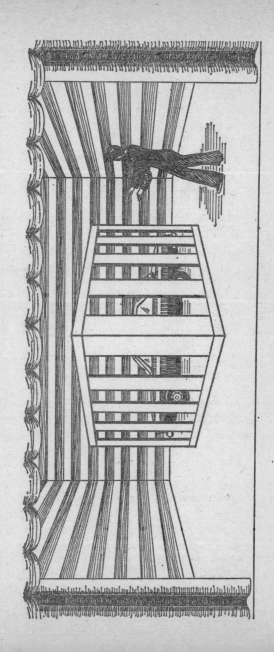

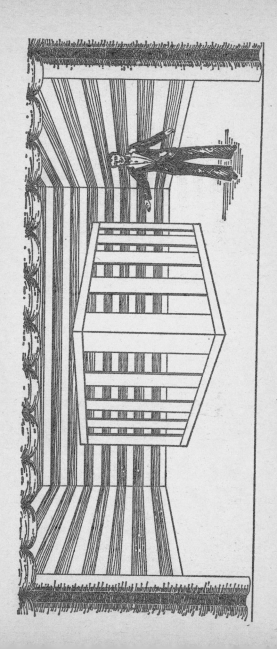

Perhaps the most stunning mirror illusion ever to be performed was Thurston's "The Disappearing Automobile." Thurston always climaxed his show with this baffling trick, which depended on vertical mirror bars that slid into place during a diversionary explosion of flash powder. The car was always borrowed from a local dealer and usually contained a "bevy of beautiful girls."

The Magic of Black Velvet

As magnificent as the illusions are with mirrors, magicians have other means of creating staggering effects. Imagine seeing this act:

The stage is set like a huge black cavern, illuminated only from the footlights and wings by glaringly bright lights. A pretty young girl is swaying back and forth on a swing while chatting with the magician, and neither seems to notice that the lower half of her body is missing.

But stranger things are yet to come. "The Half Lady" disappears with a wave of the magician's wand which suddenly takes on a life of its own. The wand struggles free from his grip and dances back and forth in space with the frustrated magician in hot pursuit. A pink vase does a somersault and sets itself on another table. Rabbits and birds appear and are gone almost as quickly. As if to taunt the magician, a skeleton puts its bones together and does a soft-shoe shuffle across the stage.

The harried conjurer finally gives up and wraps himself in a white sheet. The sheet is unwound a moment later and drops to the floor. The magician is gone!

As improbable as it may sound, all of these effects are made possible by covering the entire stage with black velvet, including the sides, backdrop, ceiling and even the floor. With bright lights in the foreground, no shadows are cast and only white or colored objects show up. Anything or anybody cloaked in matching black velvet is invisible, for dead black against dead black cannot be delineated by the human eye.

Thus, the bottom half of the young girl's body was draped in black velvet.

The dancing skeleton was actually an assistant who attached luminous white cutouts to his head-to-toe tights of black velvet. The vase, rabbits, birds and wand were manipulated by similarly clad helpers. To disappear inside the sheet, the magician wrapped himself in a matching black velvet sheet basted into the white one and faded into the background when the white one was dropped.

Invented in the 1880s by Max Auzinger and popularized by the ill-fated William Robinson (Chung Ling Soo), "Black Art" was later adapted to the motion picture to produce the uncanny effects seen in "The Invisible Man" and many other films.

Pulling a Rabbit from a Hat

Since the days they performed on street corners and at country fairs, magicians have been producing hidden objects out of their hats. Originally, magicians used their hats as protection against the weather as they traveled from town to town along the country roads.

Perhaps a wandering rabbit sneaking into the cap of a magician snoozing by the roadside first inspired what has now become the most popular magic trick.

The classic method of pulling a rabbit from a hat involves concealing a rabbit under the magician's table in a secret compartment known as a *servante*. The empty hat is displayed to the audience, and as it is placed on the table, a tiny hook on the brim catches onto the rabbit's harness and swings the animal into it, ready to be produced at the proper time. Black velvet bags filled with birds or silk handkerchiefs can also be loaded this way.

Another popular device is a hat with a fake bottom called a *feke* that swings open, in which case a mechanical rabbit is used. Called a "kicker," the phony bunny collapses to one-third its size and kicks and squirms just like the real thing when squeezed in the right places. Most magicians today use the kicker, so don't be concerned about the rabbit's tender ears—it doesn't feel a thing.

To make rabbits and other things disappear, magicians use black art wells that are part of the design of the top of the magician's table. The surface design of bold colors against black hides the wells. Several of the black squares are actually black velvet-lined holes into which the magician can push the rabbit from behind the hat while pretending to put it back inside.

The Sword Cabinet

"Torture cabinet" illusions add an element of physical danger missing from such innocuous tricks as pulling a rabbit out of a hat. They have been magic show staples since their invention in the Nineteenth Century.

In the popular "sword cabinet" effect, a female assistant enters a large, coffin-shaped box, which has been examined previously by members of the audience.

The door is locked and the magician proceeds to drive two dozen long swords through slots in the box. The audience gasps, half expecting to see blood drip from the slots, for the blades are thrust up to the hilt, and their glistening tips emerge from the other side.

There seems to be no way the woman could survive

this ordeal. Yet, when the swords are withdrawn and the door opened, she emerges free of stab wounds. The secret is that the swords are trick props. The assistant simply removes the blades as they are thrust inside. To complete the illusion, she inserts hollow sword points —concealed in a harness on her back—into the corresponding holes.

Sawing a Woman in Half

Women had been skewered with huge nails and run through with swords in various "torture cabinet" illusions of the Nineteenth Century, but it wasn't until 1921 that a British magician, P. T. Selbit, devised a way to saw a woman in half. Practically every magician since has presented a version of that effect.

Selbit's method of placing a girl in a crude, enclosed box that revealed only her head, seems tame compared with later versions. The American magician Horace Goldin created a furor of audience excitement by cutting holes in the box to expose the girl's arms and legs, and the bisected woman became the sensation of the Roaring Twenties. Before each performance, showman Goldin would hire ambulances to drive through the city with banners announcing the allegedly dangerous illusion. Nurses with stretchers and first-aid kits would wait in the theater's lobby "in case the saw slips."

The assistant who entered the box was perfectly safe, of course. She simply doubled up inside the top half of the box while another girl slipped her feet through the lower half from her hiding place inside the platform.

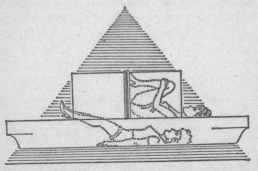

Later Goldin did away with the box altogether, and cut a girl in half through her waist on an open table with a power-driven buzz saw. Other magicians, including South America's The Great Richiardi, copied the effect and added what one reporter described "as ghastly a mess of entrails as can be found in any butcher shop."

Doug Henning presents his own version of the illusion in *The Magic Show,* in which two sections come completely apart and there is no platform. The girl lies with her knees against her chest in the first section, while mechanical feet made of plastic wiggle realistically from the bottom half.

British magician Robert Harbin has updated the sawed lady with his "Zig-Zag" illusion, also performed by Henning. An assistant enters an upright cabinet and puts her face, hands and one foot through openings in the box. After revolving the cabinet several times to show that there are no trick panels in the back, Henning proceeds to "trisect" the woman by shoving steel panels through her middle, then pulling out the center section. The secret is a closely guarded one and it is surprisingly simple. Just before the steel panels are shoved into place, the girl pushes a secret catch that opens the back of the cabinet (which is tricked after all), and she stands behind it. Moving sideways into an uncomfortable "V" position, she cranes her neck so that her face shows through an opening in the top section. Next, she stretches her right hand behind her into an opening of the center section as it is pulled out, and her left foot reaches forward through a hole in the bottom box. The girl seems to be standing inside the box, but her body is actually outside it, hidden by the center section and the cabinet frame. As you can see, the illusion requires a thin, athletic assistant who is able to endure several minutes of standing in a tortured position while continuing to smile happily.

Shooting a Woman
from a Cannon

After being subjected to outrageous simulated tortures, a female assistant may now be called upon to risk her life by being shot out of a cannon. The girl smiles innocently as she climbs into its mouth, seemingly oblivious to the danger she faces.

"Ladies and gentlemen," the magician intones solemnly. "I will now attempt to shoot this young lady

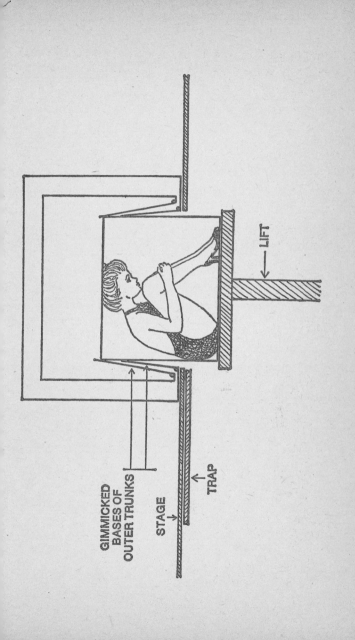

into a nest of boxes hanging from the ceiling. Please give me your full attention. A mistake in timing may prove fatal to my assistant or, possibly, to members of the audience." A drum roll begins, and the spectators look uneasily at the heavy boxes spotlighted over their heads. The girl slips deep inside the cannon. With a grand flourish, the magician ignites the charge.

POW! FLASH! The powder explodes, and the girl hurtles through the air, a human cannon ball. Lowered from their lofty perch, the nest of boxes is opened on stage. Sure enough, the girl emerges from the innermost one, her glittery costume scarcely ruffled by the split-second flight.

In reality, the girl had escaped from the cannon through an opening in the rear wheel, well before the harmless flash of powder went off. The two assistants pretended not to notice while she slipped through a trap door, and effectively misdirected attention by staring at the boxes on the ceiling.

Under the stage, the girl climbed into a small box which was loaded via another trap door into the false bottom of the nest of boxes at the moment it was placed on the stage. Since the boxes were opened from the top, the trick bottom was never noticed.

Chapter Three

MENTAL MAGIC

Mind reading, mental telepathy, prediction and other extra-sensory phenomena are the stock in trade of a special group of magicians known as mentalists. There is nothing supernatural about the abilities of these suave conjurers, however, for paranormal senses—if they exist—are not nearly reliable enough to summon up for a nightly performance.

No, mentalists must rely on normal senses honed to super-sensitivity—including a computer-like memory and excellent hearing—as well as expert sleight-of-hand to "miraculously" acquire information under seemingly impossible conditions.

Appearing to operate in the void that science cannot explain, mentalists cover up the fact that they are only conjurers. The slickest practitioner today calls himself "The Amazing Kreskin," and he is so adept at throwing us off the scent of his trickery that most of us don't even consider him a magician.

Mentalists like Kreskin present their acts as ESP experiments rather than as magic effects with expected results. "Experiments are more entertaining than demonstrations," points out magic scholar Hennings Nelms. "They give the spectators a sense of participation. They introduce an element of uncertainty which is inherently dramatic . . . Experiments are also more convincing . . . they weaken the idea that a performer is merely doing tricks."

When Kreskin appears on television and seems to be able to divine a thought from a volunteer's mind while doodling on a note pad, his self-confidence is so convincing that we say to ourselves, "So this is the ESP I've been reading about."

Take a closer look. Could his note pad be a camouflage? Can you spot any secret props in his hands?

Think about it. If he were really what he claimed to be, wouldn't he simply be able to announce what was in a person's mind without all the fooling around with envelopes, slates, note pads and the like?

Magicians have been performing mind-reading routines as long ago as 1584, when an English justice of the peace named Reginald Scot first revealed a method in his valuable survey of Elizabethan conjuring, *The Discovery of Witchcraft*. Requesting personal articles from the audience—in Scot's day a crowd gathered in the street—the magician would then ask his blindfolded confederate to identify the articles, which he would promptly do, to the amazement of all.

The secret, of course, lay in the seemingly innocuous question—which was also its answer. "Tell me, what have I here?" for instance, coded a handkerchief, while "Say what I am holding!" signaled a coin. "Do you know what I hold?" meant a comb, and so on. The code was a limited one, but good enough to fool superstitious, semi-literate audiences.

Two centuries later a German magician named Philip Breslaw came up with an improved version he described in detail in his autobiography, *Breslaw's Last Legacy*. What Breslaw had done was to expand the code and, more important, to devise, a line of patter that made the act more effective. Instead of immediately identifying the object in question, Breslaw's assistant would pause as if trying to tune into the magician's thoughts. "Yes, I am beginning to see it," she would announce dramatically. "It is something a lady never travels without. It is something in which she keeps her comb and other personal belongings. Yes, it is her handbag."

For all his ingenuity, Breslaw was a second-rate performer, and it was his more charismatic contemporary, the great Professor Pinetti, who made the routine famous. A superior showman, Pinetti adapted "thought-reading" to his already popular magic show and palmed it off as a "new discovery, no less curious than seemingly incredible."

Intimating that he possessed occult secrets of the mysterious Count Cagliostro, a practitioner of black magic who claimed to be able to turn lead into gold as well as see into the mind, Pinetti took the effect on tour and drew crowds throughout Europe. That Cagliostro was a proven fraud, murderer and thief who was languishing in prison scarcely seemed to matter, indicating that his true power, like Pinetti's, lay in manipulating minds rather than in reading them.

Ironically, Pinetti's great success led to a decline of public interest in the trick as a result of a generation of less talented imitators, many of whom made the codes laughably obvious. It took the genius of Robert-Houdin to put the mystery back into mind reading, and by doing so to turn it into the sensation of the age.

Working for months on end, Robert-Houdin took the effect out of its "Tell me, please!" rut by inventing several foolproof codes that were more extensive and subtle than any used before. To perfect his remarkable "second-sight" illusion, Robert-Houdin first embarked on a series of rigorous memory exercises with his fourteen-year-old son Emile, who was to serve as the "medium."

"My son and I passed rapidly before a toy shop, or any other displaying a variety of wares, and cast an attentive glance upon it," Robert-Houdin later explained in his *Memoires*. "A few steps further on, we drew paper and pencil from our pockets, and tried to determine which of us could describe the greater number of objects seen in passing. I must own that my son reached a perfection far greater than mine, for he could often write down forty objects, while I could scarcely reach thirty. Often feeling vexed at this defeat. I would return to the shop and verify his statement, but he rarely made a mistake."

Next, father and son spent additional months patiently memorizing and rehearsing the codes to achieve the perfection that was a hallmark of Robert-Houdin's shows. When "second sight" was finally unveiled during the winter of 1846, audiences and magicians alike were bewildered, and many believed that Robert-Houdin had broken through the psychic barrier and could genuinely transmit thoughts.

When a pocket watch was offered, for example, the blindfolded Emile not only identified it, but he told what metal it was made of, what initials were inscribed on it, if any, whether or not the case was scratched, and what time the hands indicated—even if they had been reset!

To confound skeptics who suspected that Emile could see through the blindfold, Robert Houdin accepted sealed packages, the contents of which his son promptly identified. To further confuse everyone, he dispensed with words altogether and simply rang a bell. Still Emile always came up with the correct answer.

How did Robert-Houdin convey so much information inside a few words or the tinkling of a bell? Well, it wasn't easy. Although the magician never fully disclosed his methods, his French rival, M. F. A. Gandon, provided an answer in his exposé, *Second Sight Revealed,* published three years after Robert-Houdin introduced the effect. According to Gandon, the work involved was overwhelming. Each word in a sentence spoken by Robert-Houdin to his son could mean many different things depending upon its position. With comparative few code words, then, Robert-Houdin could give clues to *hundreds* of objects.

As for being able to see inside sealed packages, Robert-Houdin simply employed a little dexterous misdirection. "I opened boxes, purses, pocket-books, etc., with great ease, and unnoticed," he later admitted, "while appearing to be engaged in something quite different. Were a sealed parcel offered me, I cut a small slit in the paper with the nail of my left thumb, which I always purposely kept long and sharp, and thus discovered what it contained."

Audiences delighted in trying to stymie the great magician by bringing in unusual articles that they themselves would find difficult to describe. Emile was always able to identify an obscure item like a twenty-gauge thread counter or to name all the foreign coins hanging from a charm bracelet, but such feats seriously taxed the code. It tended to become boring after too many repetitions.

To keep spectators on the edge of their seats, Robert-Houdin created a silent code, one that has not been improved upon to this day. Other magicians thought that a tinkling bell had something to do with it, but that was for effect only. One thing they were right about. Emile could see through the blindfold at least well enough to discern his father's outline, for Robert-Houdin's system was a subtle version of the sign language of deaf-mutes, to whom gestures are speech itself.

Moving his head up or down, to the right or left, for instance Robert-Houdin could program four different signals. Add to those, four movements of each arm and leg and he had sixteen more. Combining all of them with stance and turning movements gave him enormous possibilities of communicating information.

Whenever his "body language" code seemed to be wearing thin, Robert-Houdin would switch back to the spoken code—for which he could leave the stage and go down into the auditorium—and then back again. Compounding the mystery, the inventor-magician later incorporated a new gadget from America that was relatively unknown in France, the telegraph. Seeming to stand motionless in the center of the stage, Robert-Houdin was in reality applying the ball of his foot to a telegraph transmitter concealed under the thick carpet, and tapping out dots and dashes to a metal plate under Emile's foot.

More than once, he found a practical use for his "second-sight" act. On a particular occasion he was on tour, and a Belgian customs official refused to let him cross the border until he paid a heavy tax on his equipment. Despite Robert-Houdin's protestations that he was a professional conjurer and that the equipment was part of his act—hence, tax free—the official remained intransigent.

"Will you let us pass if I can prove to you that I am indeed what I claim to be?" the magician asked. Grunting his assent, the man continued to inspect the baggage, unaware that Robert-Houdin's hands were busy, too—picking the inspector's pockets and immediately returning what he found.

"I say, Emile," the magician called, summoning his son from across the road where he had watched the impromptu performance, "can you tell us what this gentleman has in his pockets?"

"Certainly, Papa," Emile replied without hesitation. "He has a blue-striped handkerchief . . . a green morocco spectacle case, without the spectacles . . . and a piece of sugar which the gentleman saved from his coffee." Flabbergasted, the customs man gladly let the two pass.

"Second sight" was as big a hit in New York, but it wasn't the French magician who brought it across the Atlantic. It was an imitator of Robert-Houdin, an American concert pianist who billed himself as Robert Heller and emulated his model by dying his red hair and mustache black, and affecting a French accent.

With the advent of vaudeville, as audiences grew more demanding, mentalists strived to present the old routines in new trappings. There was Mercedes who projected requests for popular songs to his piano-playing wife; Germain the Wizard whose "psychological enigma" consisted of drawing pictures coded to him; Frimini and wife, the Zancigs, the Svengalis and the Powers—all of whom answered questions sent to them "by means of telepathy."

And then there was "The Amazing Dunninger," the most famous mental wizard of his time. Dunninger revolutionized mentalism completely by doing away with codes and assistants. His deceptions were so perfect that people who remember him still scratch their heads and ask, "How did Dunninger do it?"

Born in New York in 1892, Joseph Dunninger was inspired to his exceptional career at the age of seven, when his father took him to see the great Harry Kellar's show. From then on, young Dunninger began to hang out after school at Martinka's famous magic shop, learning tricks while he learned to read and write.

By the time he was eighteen, Dunninger had mastered the whole bag of classic magic tricks, excelling at sleight-of-hand and card and coin manipulation. Ambitious and a self-promoter, Dunninger soon realized that he needed a special angle to give his routine panache, as his contemporary, Houdini, had done by becoming an escape artist. To jazz up his new act, Dunninger grew a wild mane of hair and wore a floppy, unknotted tie, an embroidered vest, spats, and completed the eccentric look with a wide-brimmed black hat.

Appearing before the Boston press in 1919, Dunninger announced to the world that he had made an earthshaking discovery. Introducing himself as president of the bogus American Psychical Society, the mentalist managed to keep a straight face while he explained that he had developed mind reading into a science. Psychic researchers and spirit mediums who claimed to be able to summon up the dearly departed were currently in the news, and Dunninger had earlier decided he could perform their feats better than they could.

Dunninger was right, of course, both about his skills of prestidigitation and the gullibility of the public. The reporters listened attentively as Dunninger extolled the future uses of his system: Policemen would know of crimes before they were committed; voters could look into the minds of crooked politicians; husbands could talk to their wives without speaking.

To back up his claims, Dunninger gave a convincing performance by asking the gentlemen of the press to write any word or number on tiny squares of paper. Next, a volunteer collected five of the slips and, according to a columnist for the Boston *Post,* Dunninger, otherwise known as "the Professor," produced an empty envelope and asked the collector to put these five scraps into it.

This the collector did with the assistance of the Professor, who tucked the papers into the envelope throwing it carelessly on the floor (flap side up). Then Dunninger asked the collector to put his foot on the envelope and keep it there.

"The Professor walked about thirty feet away and sat down behind a desk which concealed all of him below the elbows.

"To the complete astonishment of all present, he read exactly what each of the five had written on their scraps of papers. This all five admitted, and loud applause followed the demonstration."

In his haste to pat Dunninger on the back, the columnist had overlooked two important clues to the mystery, clues he had included in his story. The first was that Dunninger *helped* the volunteer tuck the slips into the envelope, and the second was that afterward, he sat down *behind* a desk. Dunninger's apparent psychic powers lay in his ability to palm undetected the five pieces of paper and substitute blank ones while his hand was inside the envelope. He then read the five slips with a quick glance under the cover of the desk. Dunninger might have been talking about himself when he once said about Thurston's levitation illusion: "The effect is easy to explain but hard to do."

Palming was only one of the many standard magic practices that Dunninger adapted to mentalism. Another was the use of that old conjurer's standby, the thumb tip, an invaluable tool for vanishing cigarettes, paper currency, billets (what professional magicians call slips of paper) and just about anything small enough to fit inside the thumb tip. Made of flesh-colored aluminum or plastic, it slips neatly over the thumb and is available at any magic shop.

As glaringly obvious as it might seem, the thumb tip is extremely effective in the hands of a master like Dunninger.

A simple variation of the thumb tip provided Dunninger with the means for one of his most baffling displays of mental telepathy. Audiences were turned into true believers when the magician correctly revealed short messages that were brought to him in sealed envelopes. Instructing a subject to tightly clasp his envelope while concentrating on its contents, Dunninger would scribble furiously on a note pad while seated at a desk. A moment later, he would order the person to tear open the envelope and reveal its contents, while he held up a piece of paper to show that he had known what the message was all along.

Actually, Dunninger didn't know it until he heard the words from his subject's mouth; the scribbling was for show. As the subject uttered the first word of the message, Dunninger was scrawling it with a thumb writer, a thumb tip with a piece of lead attached to it. Concealed by his hand and glasses, which he often toyed with "to aid in concentration," the thumb writer escaped detection since all eyes were on the subject for a few necessary seconds, while he was writing the message.

Dunninger could literally "mirror" thoughts, too. His stern manner and tall, broad-shouldered presence always intimidated his audiences and helped in the effect. Substituting blackboards for billets, Dunninger faced down challengers who had caught on to his earlier method. "Okay. Well, how do you palm a blackboard?" Dunninger responded, trying to throw his detractors off the scent.

You don't, of course. If you're Dunninger, you hand out a slate to a volunteer from the audience and ask him to write a message on it. Then you walk over to him and say, "No, please hold the slate up like this, so I can concentrate on the message." The person is probably so nervous at being onstage he doesn't notice that Dunninger has a tiny peek mirror glued to his second finger and has glimpsed the message under cover of adjusting the board. If you're Dunninger, you can read backwards as well as forwards.

In 1943 Dunninger began appearing before millions of people on radio, a perfect medium for magic that didn't depend on props or apparatus. To everyone's astonishment, Dunninger was able to address members of his studio audience by name and tell them their addresses, social security numbers and other personal data.

"Ladies and gentlemen, my work here tonight is legitimate," Dunninger announced solemnly during one broadcast. "I really can tune in upon your minds, but only if you help, only if you concentrate." An expectant hush always fell over the auditorium, and Dunninger would sit down and start doodling on a pad.

"I am receiving an impression from someone in the audience. I get the impression of fish, uh, fisher. Does that mean anything to anyone?

"Yes, that's my name," acknowledged a prim, middle-aged woman rising from her seat. After receiving her word of honor that they had never met before, Dunninger continued.

"Are you cognizant of di Lorenzo?"

"Yes, that's my fiance's name."

"Stone, what is stone?"

"My boss' name."

"And Margery?"

"My sister!"

The woman gasped even more when Dunninger told her where the wedding would take place, and if he hadn't stopped her with a wave of his hand and a "Thank you, madam," she would have filled him in on the rest of her nuptial plans. Dunninger made it seem like a bore to hear things he could read in their minds.

This astounding effect involved extensive preparation and was based on a system introduced in the late Nineteenth Century by American magician Samri S. Baldwin, who appeared professionally as The White Mahatma. A data bank was gathered on certain people who wrote for tickets, using information from their letterheads, telephone directories and newspaper morgues. If that wasn't enough, one of Dunninger's staff would call the person's house under the guise of doing a survey for a new product. At broadcast time, Dunninger had their dossiers noted on his ever-present pad of paper, along with a diagram of the location of their seats.

Ultimately many fellow magicians guessed Dunninger's secrets, but he audaciously denied their explanations even when they were right.

"If they're so damned sure they know how I do it, how come no one else is able to do it?" was Dunninger's curt reply to his critics. When an imitator did come along toward the end of his career, and even dared bill himself as "The Amazing Kreskin," Dunninger was outraged. Who was this pretender to the secrets of the great mind reader?

Kreskin was born George Kresge, Jr. in Caldwell, New Jersey in 1935—the year Dunninger read the mind of the Prince of Wales—and claims he learned magic by trying to duplicate the feats of "Mandrake the Magician," his comic-strip hero. A precocious child,

Kreskin taught himself to perform intricate stage illusions for which he also constructed the apparatus, often to the dismay of his family and friends.

Arriving home from the supermarket one afternoon, Kreskin's parents were more than startled to find their son levitated four feet above the living-room floor in a Yoga position. On another occasion Kreskin's mother happened into his room while he was trying out a new illusion and let out a scream at the sight of a light bulb moving through the air, seemingly of its own accord. Equally disturbing was Kreskin's uncanny knack of correctly guessing who was calling on the telephone before he answered it. Word eventually got around his Polish-American neighborhood that the boy possessed "the evil eye"—*porabiti* in Polish—and superstitious neighbors crossed the street whenever they passed his house.

Performing professionally at club dances and smokers while still in high school, Kreskin decided to change his name into something more exciting than George Kresge, Jr. "From Harry Kellar I took the 'k,'" he says. "From Robert-Houdin, the 'in' and added them to the beginning of my family name. Thus the stage name of Kreskin, eventually my legal name, came about."

After graduation, Kreskin put together an act based on ESP, a psychic phenomenon that had begun to generate wide public interest. Nightclub dates led to television appearances, and soon Kreskin was earning $300,000 a year, mixing parts of Dunninger's old act with variations of other tried-and-true routines. Kreskin's straight "Mr. Nice Guy" demeanor helped make his mentalism seem authentic, because a successful performance requires an audience's willing belief in the powers of the entertainer.

In perhaps his most convincing effect, Kreskin places

a $100 bill inside one of five paper bags and asks two volunteers to come on the stage. Kreskin concentrates and instructs them to set fire to any two of the bags and to take another two back to their seats. The remaining bag always contains the $100 bill.

Despite Kreskin's pretension of supernormal powers, how this illusion is done is quite simple. Kreskin palms the $100, and when he tears open the remaining bag, he triumphantly shows the $100 bill "emerging" from the bag.

Television gave Kreskin the opportunity to display for a wide audience some of his standard tricks, such as the linking together of wedding bands collected from members of the audience. This is merely a small-scale version of the well-known Chinese linking rings trick. Kreskin uses his own ring set consisting of seven pre-linked metal hoops and one key hoop with a cut in it. Since most wedding bands look alike, Kreskin has only to substitute the ones he has collected for his own set, keeping the most recognizable one from the audience to place inside the first, cut, link of his pre-linked rings.

Kreskin performs the paper billet hoax, too, with the help of a little gadget used for mind reading that is a staple in magic stores. In the paper billet hoax, which Dunninger did so skillfully, the magician "miraculously" reveals what a subject has secretly written on a piece of paper. But Kreskin lays the groundwork for his telepathy before showtime by asking his subjects to write down the thought they will try to transmit to him. At no time does he touch the billet. The guests pocket the slips to be used as proof later, but return the clipboard Kreskin gave them to write on. A Canadian psychic researcher caught onto this one quickly.

"It's a trick clipboard," explains Allen Spraggett, who writes a syndicated column on ESP. "The performer asks his guest to write down his secret on a single sheet of paper on the board. The guest takes the paper, leaving only the clipboard behind and says nothing. What he doesn't know is that the hard top of the clipboard is carbonned. You peel the top back to see a copy of what was written. The performer has the answer before he goes onstage."

Another Kreskin deception exposed by Spraggett involves a padlock and ten different keys. Handing out the keys to volunteers from the audience, Kreskin instructs them to line up and try to open the lock. None of the keys works except the last one.

Next, the magician dumps the keys into a bowl, chains and padlocks a volunteer and leaves the theater. A few minutes later, he telephones and orders, say, volunteer number six to select randomly one of the keys and stand by. The master of ceremonies then collects the remaining keys, seals them inside an envelope and drops the envelope into a mailbox. Though the odds are nine to one against it, the key always opens the padlock and releases the chained man.

According to Spraggett, "It's very simple, actually. The one key that opens the lock is the last one of the bunch that is tried. What is does is trigger a mechanism in the lock which enables all the other keys to open it. The performer can't possibly lose."

In 1973, Dunninger, too old and frail to continue performing, launched an attack against Kreskin, who had never acknowledged his debt to the master mentalist. Taking him to task in his book, *Dunninger's Secrets* —which gave away as few secrets as Kreskin's book, *The Amazing World of Kreskin*—he claimed to reveal the younger mentalist's "inferior" techniques.

"In another TV appearance, the Mighty Marvel (Kreskin) went groping around the studio blindfolded,"

Dunninger wrote, "using some secret sense to track down a large toy balloon that a spectator was holding on a string. Finally getting his bearings, the MM bore down upon his prey, made a dramatic gesture with a long pin that he carried, and stabbed the balloon so perfectly that it went 'POW'—just like that, informing the rapt viewers that another modern miracle had been achieved in the name of science and ESP. Of course the MM wore his own blindfold, because he hadn't asked people to bring their own blindfolds.

"His own, when drawn tight, was thin enough to see through, but he didn't waste time letting people try it for themselves. He stalled long enough during the balloon hunt to bow off, blindfold and all, after accomplishing his aim. It never occurred to anyone to ask why this Marvel who claimed the ability to find tiny objects hidden almost anywhere, needed an inflated balloon as a target when working blindfolded. The reason was, he couldn't see anything smaller without his glasses. If he'd worn them under his blindfold, the act would have looked even funnier that it was."

To be fair, despite Dunninger's opinion, Kreskin may have found the balloon using a more difficult method known as muscle reading, which operates on the same principles as a lie detector. Kreskin often winds up his act with this exciting effect, which is closely related to the game of "hot and cold."

At the beginning of this routine, Kreskin announces to the audience that his host has hidden his paycheck somewhere on the premises, and that if he doesn't find it later, he will forfeit the money. Money being one of the strongest human motivations, the self-challenge produces considerable tension. But Kreskin always finds it, even if the check is hidden inside a book binding, under a toilet seat or frozen inside an ice-cube tray.

The solution to this marvelous effect has less to do with magic than a knowledge of psychology and a sensitive touch. Before starting his search, Kreskin instructs his host to visualize his instructions as the magician follows him around the room. "Consciously think, 'This way,' or 'no it's over here' or 'higher,' " Kreskin tells him. "But don't say it out loud."

Holding his employer's arm, Kreskin takes him around the room, feeling for his involuntary muscle reflexes. A slight restraining motion tells Kreskin that he is headed in the wrong direction; no resistance indicates he is getting warmer, and eventually he finds the money.

The concept of "reading" muscles was first enunciated by scientists in the nineteenth century. Evolutionist Charles Darwin had pointed out that when you want someone to move in a certain direction, it is nearly impossible to control your own unconscious movement in that direction. The principle came to be termed motor automatism or ideo-motor behavior by psychologists, and it is said to account for such automatic behavior as the moving of a pointer on a Ouija board, or even our tendency to move with players at a tennis match.

Kreskin also applies this principle to a table-turning trick that results from nervous tension built up by a group of people who place their hands on a table and will it to move. You can try this experiment yourself with the help of three friends and a card table. Seated at the table, rest your hands near the center of the top, spread them, and touch your little fingers to the little fingers of the persons on either side of you. Make sure that all four of you are touching or the trick won't work.

Now, concentrate on willing the table to move and do not speak. A dynamic tension will eventually build up (it may take a while at first) and the table will move, tilt, or even topple over. The effect seems magical, but it is actually the result of physical stress triggered by mental concentration.

There may be more mysterious means of moving inanimate objects, however, some of which defy logical explanation. But more about that in the next chapter.

Chapter Four

THE UNEXPLAINED:
MAGIC AND ESP

Of all the magicians performing today, the most controversial is a young Israeli "psychic" named Uri Geller. Since journeying from the land of Biblical miracles in 1972, Geller has achieved international fame by exhibiting his talents throughout the Western world on television, in nightclubs, on lecture stages and at universities.

At the touch of Geller's hands, nails, keys, and silverware bend, broken watches start keeping time and working ones stop, flowers wilt, and sounds disappear from magnetic tapes. Moreover, Geller is able to receive and project thoughts, duplicate drawings in sealed envelopes, correctly call the fall of dice in a closed box and even drive a car while blindfolded!

Such marvels are all in a day's work for conjurers, but what separates Geller from other entertainers is the claim that his magic is *genuine* and not a result of props, sleight-of-hand, misdirection and other magic techniques. "I am not a conjurer," Geller insists. "There is no illusion in what I do. It is all real."

As they had with Dunninger and Kreskin, professional magicians have accused Geller of misrepresenting himself as a psychic superman for the sake of building a highly profitable career. "Geller is nothing more than a trickster," asserts Melbourne Christopher, chairman of the Psychic Investigation Committee of the Society of American Magicians, which conducted a preliminary investigation of Geller. "He is no more genuine than a four-dollar bill. Any skilled magician can duplicate his deceptions." But those who have heard about Geller's amazing background have their doubts.

He was born in Tel Aviv on December 20, 1946. According to Geller, his "energy forces" were a result of a strange light that attacked him at the age of three or four while playing in an isolated garden across the street from his home. The light knocked him unconscious, and when he awoke several hours later, he began to exhibit strange and frightening powers.

For one thing, Geller could read his mother's thoughts and tell her how much money she had won or lost at her weekly card game. For another, young Uri could move the hands of his watch just by thinking about it. In grade school, Geller recalls, "I noticed that I'd be wishing that it was 3:00—the time that school let out—only to look down at my watch to see that the hands had moved to that hour, even though it was much earlier. I complained to my mother about the wristwatch being broken; she examined it and said there was nothing wrong. But it continued to happen, so one day in class I took it off and held it in my hands, watching it closely. I began to notice that the watch hands would change their positions almost instantaneously—like dematerializing from one hour to another."

Geller soon put his psychic abilities to a practical use by reading the minds of the brightest students in class and copying their answers to tests, complete with their mistakes. The teachers accused him of cheating but couldn't prove it since Geller was sitting across the room from the students whose test papers matched his own.

One teacher contacted Geller's parents, who were already concerned with their son's uncanny and often embarrassing ability to bend knives and forks at home and in restaurants. They warned him to "cut out" the trickery and threatened to send him to a psychiatrist. From then on Geller fought to control the powers. Whenever they got out of hand, Geller would make a joke of it, telling friends and relatives that they were only tricks lest they think him crazy.

While serving in the Israeli Army (he was wounded in the Six-Day War with Egypt), Geller finally found an appreciative audience among his buddies, for whom he staged impromptu mind-reading and spoon-bending shows. Discharged, the tall, dark, and handsome Geller worked for a time as a model, and in 1969 became a professional conjurer.

"To support myself I had become a stage magician," explains Geller. "But when I dropped the effects and claimed my powers were genuine and not the result of sleight-of-hand, the newspapers branded me a trickster."

By the end of 1971, Geller had generated enough controversy to become famous in Israel and Europe and had come to the attention of the noted parapsychologist and electronics expert, Dr. Andrija Puharich. Always on the lookout for a psychic superman, Dr. Puharich had previously sponsored the career of Peter Hurkos, the Dutch clairvoyant who allegedly possesses the power to identify murderers from vibrations of clues found at the scene of the crime.

Puharich brought Geller to the United States and booked him on television talk shows. Viewers of Merv Griffin and Mike Douglas watched in awe as Geller rubbed perfectly straight six-inch spikes between his fingers and made them bend, then correctly reproduced drawings in sealed envelopes and, by passing his hands over them, located the one can in ten that contained a hidden object.

When the latter feat failed to come off on Johnny Carson's show, American magicians cried "fraud," as did Carson, once a magician himself. To rule out trickery, Carson had placed the cans on a sturdy table, and he refused to let Geller touch the table when he passed his hands over the cans. Naturally, one can was heavier than the others and would vibrate differently if the table were jarred. Carson says it seemed to him that Geller was stamping his feet very hard in time to the music during the station breaks in order to jar the cans.

A conjurer who has made an avocation of debunking Geller by duplicating nearly all his magic feats, the Amazing Randi claims he caught on to Geller's trickery while posing as a reporter during a *Time* magazine interview. After Geller left, Randi demonstrated how it is possible to substitute one of the nails selected by his audience with a previously bent, palmed one. The bent nail is displayed at an angle that conceals the bend, which appears by slowly turning it on the pretext of rubbing it. The effect is that the audience appears to see the nail bend before their eyes.

When *Time* staffers offered Randi keys from their own pockets and a spoon from the company cafeteria, he bent those, too. "I simply misdirected their attention," explains Randi, "and while they were looking elsewhere I bent a key against the leg of my chair, under a table or anything else that was handy. You can do the same with spoons, and you can bend them with your fingers if your hand is strong enough."

Melbourne Christopher claims that Geller uses a corrosive chemical to weaken the stems of the tableware, and a physicist from England's Bristol University believes that Geller has the objects made up of a recently developed alloy of nickel and titanium, called Nitinol. The metal is easily bent but when heated (even by rubbing) the metal springs back to its original shape. Geller, of course, dismisses these theories and states that he can bend any metal including Nitinol.

No one is quite sure how Geller manages to start and stop wristwatches by passing his hands over them, although Christopher believes it may be the result of a palmed magnet. "Look, we don't claim to know how he does all of his tricks," says Randi. "He's good, very good, and magicians never reveal their secrets."

During the *Time* session, Randi also duplicated the Geller feat of reproducing drawings made by volunteers by secretly slitting open the envelopes in which they were concealed and getting a quick look at them. On another occasion, Randi simply watched the movement of the drawer from across the room, "pencil reading" what was being put on paper. The technique is well known to magicians, and part of the training program for C.I.A. recruits. The conclusion of the *Time* article was that Geller was nothing more than "a questionable nightclub magician."

To the Society of American Magicians, Geller's avoidance of its challenge for a performance before a panel of magicians is prima facie proof of his charlatanism. Looking down his nose at the skeptical conjurers, Geller surprised them by accepting instead an invitation to be tested by California's prestigious Stanford Research Institute, one of America's leading "think tanks." "I'll let the scientists figure out what it is I've got," explained Geller.

At S.R.I., Geller successfully worked most of his repertoire of miracles:

* He predicted the throw of dice eight times in a row against odds of a million to one (precognition).
* He guessed twelve times in a row which of ten aluminum cans contained hidden objects, against odds of a trillion to one (clairvoyance).
* He transmitted to the Institute's vice president a number that the later had in his mind (telepathy).
* He bent a laboratory balance under a bell jar without touching it (psychokinesis).
* He reproduced seven of nine drawings that were selected by computer outside the sealed, metal-lined room in which he sat.

Yet even before the S.R.I.'s findings were released, rumblings were heard about the Institute's "cheat-proof" precautions. Ray Hyman, a psychology professor at the University of Oregon, observed several of the tests and accused S.R.I. of "incredible sloppiness." He claimed that he caught Geller in outright deceptions. In one case, Hyman says, Geller asked a researcher to write down a number from one to ten and to attempt to transmit it to him telepathically. Geller put his hands over his eyes as the man wrote, but Hyman observed that they were visible through his fingers as he watched the motions of the pencil.

As Randi points out, the purpose of the art of magic is to make people believe they have seen the impossible without being able to figure out how it was done. "And scientists are the easiest people to fool," Randi says. "They look for complicated explanations, and the explanations are always simple. The people who are hardest to fool are children, because they look at what they're not supposed to. Scientists are pushovers."

The S.R.I. stands by its findings, nevertheless, guarding its reputation as an arbiter of scientific discoveries that does $70,000,000 worth of business with both the government and private industry.

Besides lending credence to Geller's claims, the Stanford Research Institute's findings boosted the reputation of parapsychology in general. Parapsychology is the study of telepathy, clairvoyance, thought transference and other forms of extra-sensory perception that science cannot explain. For decades parapsychologists had sought to be recognized, and now here was one of the bastions of establishment science—which had so often dismissed their research as a joke—conceding the possibility of the existence of magical powers that will not yield to rational explanation.

Have you ever asked yourself if you might possess any of the "extrasensory" powers claimed by Uri Geller? According to parapsychologists, the "psi" factor, an innate capacity of the mind for extrasensory perception, operates in many of us. Telepathic impressions, for instance, are said to be constantly bombarding our minds. Few make it through to consciousness, however, because we are too busy with the problems of the day to allow them to penetrate. Unless a psychic impression is particularly strong, we are most likely to receive it in moments of deep relaxation, at bedtime or in dreams.

If you can answer yes to one or more of the questions that follow, you may be among the 10% who supposedly possess psi power:

* Have you ever thought of a loved one, only to have that person telephone you seconds or minutes after the thought?
* When the telephone rings, do you often know

who is on the other end of the line before you pick up the receiver?

* Have you ever had a vivid dream that later became reality?
* Have you ever had a premonition about a loved one or an event, and then had the premonition come true?

Of course, rational explanations have to be ruled out before identifying something as paranormal. Knowing that a certain person is likely to telephone you at a certain time is just good reasoning, not mental telepathy. And guessing who is on the line several times in a row may be merely the result of the mathematical laws of probability, like a gambler's lucky streak.

And prophetic dreams and premonitions may be merely a function of your subconscious mind, that part of your intelligence which psychologists say is most often released during sleep. A premonition that a relative will die, soon followed by the event, may be a result of noticing signs of the person's declining condition and/or things you may have heard. You may have put this depressing information out of your conscious mind, only to have filed it away subconsciously.

Furthermore, many people have premonitions from time to time that do not come true. Professional "seer" Jeane Dixon has built a lucrative career based on her "gift of prophecy." She correctly predicted in the *Parade* newspaper supplement of May 13, 1956 that "a Democratic President elected in 1960 will be assassinated." Few of us are aware, however, of Mrs. Dixon's many failures, including her later contradictory forecast that Richard Nixon would defeat John F. Kennedy in the 1960 presidential election. In 1969 newspaper editors saved Mrs. Dixon (and themselves) from public embarrassment by hastily deleting from her syndicated column a prediction that President Kennedy's widow would never remarry. Earlier that day Jackie Kennedy had become Mrs. Aristotle Onassis.

Jeane Dixon's "gift" may be genuine ESP, but many of her accurate prophecies could just as easily be a result of educated guesswork. Her prediction that actress Marilyn Monroe would one day take her own life is a case in point as is her 1952 prediction of the race riots of 1963 and 1964. Many informed people knew that the Hollywood star was suicidal, and a little historical research would reveal to anyone that race riots have occurred in the United States in this century roughly every twenty-two years.

Predicting the future on a *one-to-one* level is the business of an underworld of fake ESP consultants who call themselves fortune tellers, gypsy tea-leaf readers and palmists. These are con artists who win the confidence of gullible clients by looking into crystal balls, tea dregs and hand wrinkles. But the most talented of these practitioners can sometimes tell their dupes amazingly accurate facts about themselves, a "psychic" feat that relies on a little-known magician's art called "cold reading."

The technique is based on principles of psychology and involves the reading of a person's body language: how he is dressed and groomed and what his posture, movements and gestures reveal. The client's expression tells the cold reader if his guess is accurate, and if not he switches to another approach, his true purpose obscured in his or her mysterious line of patter.

The client is unaware that the fortune teller's statements are actually questions to which the client is supplying the answers. Feeding back the information acquired in this way, the fortune teller convinces the client that he can see into the past, and then he proceeds with the future. "Yes, you will get the job," or "Yes, you will marry him," the charlatan predicts, telling the "sucker" what he or she wants to hear.

The world of psychics has always had its share of fakers—and many have become famous. The rage of the Victorian era, for example, was spiritualism. Its superstars were the three Fox sisters, who generated as much controversy then as Uri Geller does today. Surfacing with their "gift" in 1848, the teen-aged girls drew huge crowds to the family home in Hydesville, New York, where they demonstrated their incredible ability to ask questions of the spirits of the dearly departed and to receive answers in the form of rapping sounds.

Soon the United States, England and Europe were inundated with mediums who collected sizable fees by convincing the gullible that they were able to contact deceased relatives and loved ones through their superior psychic talents. Attending seances became fashionable and remained so even after Margaret Fox admitted that the spirit rappings came from their double-jointed toes, which made loud cracking sounds when the girls bent them.

Among other frauds were the Davenport brothers, Ira and William, who became music-hall headliners on the strength of their frighteningly realistic cabinet seances. Their hands securely bound behind them to their feet, the brothers were locked facing each other in a large wardrobe cabinet (the spirits would only consent to appear in total darkness) hung wth guitars, bells, tambourines and other musical instruments. Once the cabinet doors were shut, ghostly music began to emanate from inside, and loud raps were heard. The cabinet doors were flung open several times and the brothers were seen still tied, the instruments in their original positions—proof that spirits were doing the playing.

The Davenport brothers' secret lay in their ability to obtain slack in the rope while being tied—a simple escape trick—which enabled them to slip one of their hands in and out of the loops.

As recently as the 1920s, despite all the exposés, a large segment of the public still seemed to believe that spirit mediums were truly able to communicate with the dead. The *Scientific American* offered a prize of $2,500 to any medium who could pass a series of tests devised by its committee, one of whose members was the highly skeptical Harry Houdini. Noting that many still believed Houdini's incredible escapes were due to supernatural powers—despite his protestations to the contrary— Houdini welcomed the opportunity to unmask the frauds and to educate a guillible public. Not one of the "psychics" could lay claim to the money after Houdini had finished with him, but at least one came close.

Mina Crandon was the beautiful socialite wife of a Boston surgeon who had risen to national prominence as "Margery" the medium, through whom her deceased brother, Walter, brought forth spirits of the netherworld. "Walter" was given to speaking in obscenities that no lady of the era would use, much less know about; and this was offered as an additional proof of Margery's veracity.

Mrs. Crandon had passed all of the preliminary tests of the *Scientific American* when Houdini arrived at her Boston home one hot July night in 1924 to administer his own test. Houdini sat at her left and placed the bell box (a spiritualist fixture that consists of a battery-operated bell that rings at the slightest ghostly pressure) under his chair. Then he clasped Mrs. Crandon's hand and placed his right foot over her left. The hands of those attending the scene were linked around the table, and the room was plunged into total darkness.

The bell rang several times during the next hour; the spirits levitated a megaphone, threw it across the room, and then toppled a screen, while "Walter" spoke in Mrs. Crandon's strangely guttural voice and vaguely described the spirit world. The seance seemed genuine enough, but Houdini had proof that it wasn't.

In preparation Houdini had sensitized his right leg the day before by wearing a tight rubber surgical bandage until the skin became tender. Just before the lights went out Houdini had rolled up his trouser leg so that he could detect small leg motions that might go undetected under heavy material. Little by little Houdini could feel Mrs. Crandon's leg slowly inching forward to ring the bell. Mrs. Crandon's husband held on to her right hand, enabling her to let go and reach for the megaphone and, according to Houdini, "place it on her head duncecap fashion [and] snap [it] off her head in any direction requested." The room was so dark no one could see her trickery. Being an accomplished athlete, Margery was also able to topple the screen behind her with a deft kick of her right foot, without disturbing her position, but Houdini could feel "her body give and sway as though she had made a vigorous lunge."

The dead giveaway came during another seance when "Walter" called for everyone to move back from the table so that he could levitate it. The table rose into the air and Houdini suddenly reached his hand under it. He banged into Mrs. Crandon's head! Unseen by the other members of the seance, Margery had ducked underneath the table to "levitate" it. "I do not think she was more surprised than I," Houdini recalled. "She then said something about losing hairpins, and after the seance, her hair was loosened. This was done for effect and to offset my discovery."

After Houdini died on Halloween afternoon in 1926, the extent of his interest in spiritualism became better known. Like many others before him, Houdini had been searching for a medium who could prove the existence of a spirit life after death. Until her own death in 1943, Beatrice Houdini consulted hundreds of mediums in the hope that one of them would be able to repeat the secret code and the private words that her beloved husband had told her would prove he was communicating with her. In life Houdini had vowed to come back to her if the spirit world truly existed, but the bridge was never gapped, and Houdini's assessment of spirit mediums still stands: "Of all the mediums I have encountered, not one of them has satisfied me with the genuineness of psychical phenomena."

Two years after Houdini's death, a young psychologist and former divinity student named Joseph Banks Rhine brought psychic research into a modern scientific setting when he founded the Parapsychology Laboratory at Duke University in North Carolina. Instead of attempting to prove and fathom demonstrations of allegedly gifted individuals such as mediums, Rhine investigated the phenomena itself to determine to what extent ordinary individuals might possess unrealized paranormal powers.

Rhine first developed a viable terminology, replacing the older term, "psychic research," with the more accurate "parapsychology" and identifying the power being studied as "psi."

Rhine tested students and staff as well as many volunteers for their ability to identify cards randomly selected by a tester. The results of thousands of tests did indicate that many ordinary people were in possession of paranormal faculties, although critics argued that since the deck Rhine used contained only five different cards, luck, and not ESP, accounted for the successful guessing.

Nevertheless, by the 1940s Rhine's concept of ESP was accepted as a valid possibility by a majority of the public, and dozens of conjurers followed Joseph Dunninger's lead and added ESP effects to their mentalist acts. An enterprising young Pakistani named Kuda Bux jumped on the psi bandwagon to earn fleeting fame by passing himself off as an "eyeless seer." He pedaled confidently through the world's capitals on a bicycle while his eyes were covered with bread dough and a thick blindfold.

Bux never admitted to trickery, but the fact has been duplicated by countless conjurers, including Uri Geller, who drives a car blindfolded. Corinda's magic textbook, *Thirteen Steps to Mentalism,* describes several methods of the "blindfold street drive," all of which depend upon seeing through or under the blindfold. The effect works on the curiously inverse principle that the more material used, the easier the cheating. Dough plasters adhere to cloth better than they do to skin. Under the guise of adjusting the blindfold while it is being applied, the "seer" presses the cloth into the dough. It is a simple matter to slide the dough and the inner covering down the cheeks, making it possible to peer through the remaining gauzy layers. Many types of cloth that look opaque from a distance can actually be seen through when held against the eyes.

A few years after Kuda Bux retired and opened a business with his considerable earnings, reports of other, verified forms of eyeless sight began to trickle through the Iron Curtain from Russia. Though less sensational than Bux's alleged feat, several Soviet women were discovered to possess the paranormal ability to "read" colors with their fingertips while blindfolded.

Spurred on by the Soviet Union's announcement that it had allotted $14,000,000 yearly for parapsychological research, the United States Defense Department added a magical dimension to the Cold War and began its own research. "The Joint Chiefs of Staff," reported Newsweek in October, 1956, ". . . are looking into the possibility of using ESP not only to read the minds of Soviet leaders but to influence their thinking by long-range thought control."

By the time Uri Geller arrived on the scene, world interest in parapsychology was at an all-time high. Scientists had become less tradition-bound as they discovered things that literally boggled the mind: Black holes—empty voids—that exist in the universe; particles that travel faster than the speed of light; antimatter, and quasar stars. In 1969, noted anthropologist Margaret Mead successfully argued for the admission of the Parapsychology Association in the august American Association for the Advancement of Science by pointing out that "The whole history of scientific advancement is full of scientists investigating phenomena that the Establishment did not believe were there."

Chapter Five

MAGIC ON THE SCREEN

Like conjuring, movies and television are entertainments that trick us into believing we see impossible things. On the screen an illusionary trip to outer space seems as real as the view we see of the sky each day from our own windows; the miracles described in the Bible can be experienced in detail, and a giant ape who never existed is able to climb to the top of the Empire State Building.

Under the spell of this magic, so powerful and complete, we rarely remember that the images flickering before us with all the semblance of life aren't moving at all.

What we see while watching a movie is a series of still photographs projected at a steady speed of twenty-four frames per second. Each photograph (or frame) stops on the screen just long enough to fix the image on the eye before the next picture takes its place. And the only moving part of a television screen is a flying spot of electricity known as a scanner. Moving down and across the picture tube (in the same way you are reading this book), the scanner draws a picture on thousands of light-producing phosphor dots that coat the inside of the screen. Each complete scan follows the previous one about thirty times a second, just like the pictures on a strip of movie film.

A curious property of the eye, called persistence of vision, holds the previous image on the retina even while the next one is hitting it, fooling us into perceiving a smooth, lifelike motion. You can demonstrate this to yourself with a pencil and a small, gum-edged pad of paper. Draw a stick figure of a person walking on the last page in the bottom corner and continue drawing it on each top page, changing its position slightly as it moves forward. Then flip back the pages and watch your animated cartoon move forward. With practice you can even make the figure seem to run.

Supplying the magic for the optical illusions that are movies and television is a small army of unheralded wizards called special effects men. Most of their work is on film because it is more easily manipulated than videotape.

"What we do is to make photographable anything that a scriptwriter's imagination can come up with," explains Danny Lee, special effects boss at Walt Disney Studios. "All it takes is mechanical ability, a knowledge of hydraulics, explosives and no acquaintance with the word *impossible*."

Appropriately enough, the first special effects man was a professional magician, George Méliès, who was famous in France as the twenty-five-year-old owner and star attraction of the Theatre Robert-Houdin, the palace of magic built by the legendary French conjurer nearly fifty years before.

One afternoon in 1895 while searching for new stage effects, Méliès investigated a novelty entertainment that had recently captured the public's fancy. Two enterprising young inventors, the Lumière brothers, had seemingly achieved the impossible by adding a dimension of lifelike movement to the familiar "magic lantern" slide shows which had been around even before the invention of the photograph. Newspaper critics were unimpressed, however, and dismissed this revolutionary new entertainment as "flickering tintypes" and "cheap shows for cheap people."

Although undaunted by negative press reports, Méliès may have had second thoughts as he took a seat in the Lumière brothers' dingy little theater, actually the basement of a sidewalk cafe. As the houselights dimmed, Méliès heard a noise like a coffee grinder and watched luminous white blotches suddenly break out on a large piece of canvas stretched across the makeshift stage. Gradually, as the projectionist focused the hand-cranked *Cinematographe,* the blotches coalesced into the image of an oncoming train.

An awed hush fell over the audience witnessing this marvel. Astonishment quickly gave way to terror, however, as the train steamed ever closer. Finally, just as the locomotive seemed about to hurtle off the screen and into their laps, the audience could take no more. Several screaming viewers bolted for the door while others escaped by fainting.

The magician watched with delight as adults with normal reactions and intelligence behaved like six-year-olds. If they had had time to think, perhaps the spectators' common sense would have preserved their dignity. As it was, they had been taken by surprise with a form of trickery they neither understood nor had previously seen.

Méliès knew well that these elements were key ingredients for a successful magic show, and he offered to buy the Lumière brothers' apparatus for his own theater.

"Not even for 10,000 *francs, Monsieur,*" came the reply. Determined to add this fantastic new illusion to his repertoire, Méliès played a dirty trick not uncommon to magicians: He bought a copy from an unscrupulous inventor who had counterfeited the machine.

Like a camera buff infatuated with his new super-8, Méliès began filming practically anything that moved in order to feature it in his magic act, until he had the happy accident that is now part of movie history. Photographing a horse-drawn city bus driving past the Paris Opera, Méliès' camera jammed. Muttering under his breath, he recranked the bulky instrument, but by the time he was able to continue shooting, the bus had driven by, and a hearse stood in its place.

Viewing the reel later proved to be a revelation for Méliès. On the screen his accidental double exposure had magically transformed the bus into a hearse. His magician's imagination immediately set to work exploiting all the trick possibilities of a movie camera, and he invented other more startling effects. With the help of trapdoors, mirrors, levitation wires and other equipment Robert-Houdin had built into the theater, Méliès was able to film illusions that were impossible to perform onstage.

On film Méliès could make a woman disappear from the screen simply by stopping the camera and having her step out of camera range. The flesh of a man could be made to dissolve from his bones by overlapping shots of an actor, a medical school dummy and a skeleton. Years later this "stop-motion" technique would make possible such movies as *King Kong* and Walt Disney's animated cartoon films.

On film, Méliès' head could leave his body, float in the air and multiply into many heads. Thanks to the magic of double exposures, ghostly presence could be summoned from their corpses to walk through walls. Generations later, moviegoers would still thrill to these basic screen illusions in such films as *Dracula, The Invisible Man* and *The Exorcist.*

Méliès even invented a visual language that movies and television use to this day. To suggest the passage of time Méliès devised the fade-in and the fade-out, which is the gradual lightening or darkening of the beginning or end of a new scene. To suggest a flashback to the past or the beginning of a dream, Méliès came up with the dissolve, which is a double-exposed transition of the end of one scene over the beginning of another.

Of his more than 1,500 movies, *A Trip to the Moon* was Méliès' most popular and one of the few that still exist. In the then-mammoth sixteen-minute spectacle—so obviously shot on the stage of Méliès' theater, against painted backdrops—a group of Victorian astronauts are loaded into a gigantic rocket that is fired into the eye of the Man in the Moon, whose jolly face grimaces in pain. After being greeted by buxom moon-maidens who can fly, the earthlings are menaced by popeyed, papier-mâché-helmeted "Selenites." Outnumbered by the Selenites, whose ranks are increased by the use of parallel mirrors, the men escape back to earth, their business suits and ties scarcely ruffled by the experience.

Despite his great influence on screen magic, the good-natured Méliès didn't make much money at it. Never a good businessman, Méliès sold his films outright instead of renting them, allowing other exhibitors to get rich from repeated admissions charges. By the end of the First World War, audience tastes had changed, and Méliès went bankrupt trying to revive his trick movies. Virtually forgotten by the industry he had helped to create, the foremost magician of the screen ended his days peddling toys on the streets of Paris.

Ironically, one of Méliès' disciples proved to be instrumental in making the work of the great pioneer obsolete. He was a young American, Edwin S. Porter, who had figured out many of the master's secrets while working as a projectionist with a traveling tent show that featured the Frenchman's movies.

Porter combined what he had learned with some original trickery in his trend-setting 1903 opus, *The Great Train Robbery*. Realizing that audiences were tiring of trickery for its own sake and wanted movies that offered dramatic plots and realistic action, Porter turned his magic to the purely practical purpose of telling a story of bandits holding up a train.

Operating on a shoestring budget, Porter invented the ingenious "matte" technique that is now standard film practice. Born of economic necessity, the effect was created for a scene that called for a train to steam past the open window of a telegraph office. To enable the train to be put into the window later, Porter placed a cardboard cutout "matte" in the shape of the window inside the camera lens, then shot the studio scene and rewound the film. Later, when it was convenient, Porter inserted a matching "counter-matte," that blacked out the studio scene and went out to the suburbs and filled in the unexposed "window" with a moving train. The separate double exposure created the illusion that the two images were part of the same scene.

Porter was one of the first directors to cut costs by filming a story out of sequence, scheduling all the studio shots the first three days and the locations shots the next three. Working this way, Porter was able to make it look as if he had used scores of actors when, in reality, he had hired less than a dozen. "I played everything but the horse," recalled Bronco Billy Anderson—the John Wayne of his day—who got his start in *The Great Train Robbery*. "I was a passenger on the train who was killed, and I was also the bandit who shot him. I even doubled as a fireman who went after the bandit in the caboose."

Splicing together the pieces of film shot at different times and different places in order to tell a coherent story, Porter discovered a way to play tricks with time that added to the illusion of reality. Cross-cutting from reactions of the passengers to actions of the bandits and then to the reactions of the train engineer, Porter made it possible to experience the robbery from every point of view. This stretched out the time it would take for such an event to happen, but made the robbery more gripping to see on the screen than it would be in real life. The result was 450 feet of celluloid excitement that delighted movie-goers and launched an enduring film genre: a Western with a chase.

Other filmmakers continued to refine the matte technique, sometimes with unintentionally ridiculous results. Hollywood cameraman Charles Rosher had such a steady hand that he was actually able to hold a matte inside the lens and follow the movements of Mary Pickford—the "Sweetheart of the Silent Screen"—playing a dual role in *Little Lord Fauntleroy*.

"The double exposures are the finest that have ever been made in the history of the business," applauded a 1925 movie magazine reviewer, concurring that two Marys were better than one. "When Mary Pickford kisses herself as 'Deariest', and hugs herself, and when both characters walk off together, one ahead of the other . . . well, it's almost uncanny. Hats off to Rosher."

Less obvious but more enduring in the trickery cooked up by A. Arnold Gillespie for the first version of *Ben-Hur*, also released in 1925. Realizing that perspective disappears on the flat, two-dimensional screen, Gillespie

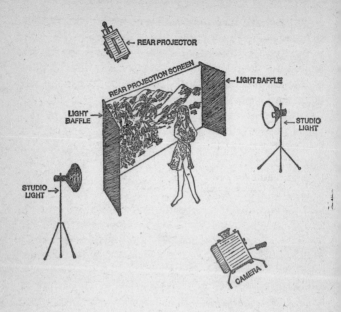

built a thirty-foot-high set (which was miniature in name only) of the imposing arena of the ancient Circus Maximus, and placed it directly behind the full-scale chariot race track. As the horses galloped by, 10,000 tiny human figures stood up and waved at the pull of a string. Although the miniature was only a few feet in back of the charioteers, the effect was of a background space larger than a football field.

With the advent of sound came a new background process that, at the flick of a switch, could transport actors sitting in a Hollywood studio to an African jungle, a Paris cafe or a moving taxi. The secret was something called rear projection. As the name suggests, it is a system of projecting moving background scenery onto a translucent screen from behind the live actors.

Director Alfred Hitchcock made a particularly effective use of this technique for a thrilling plane crash in *Foreign Correspondent* (1940). Placing the camera behind the shoulders of the two actors playing the pilots of the airliner, Hitchcock filmed the ocean coming closer and closer via a rear-projection screen placed on the other side of the cockpit. At the moment of supposed impact, Hitchcock released a tank of water that broke through the thin screen and flooded the set. The screen was destroyed so quickly that it was impossible to tell it had ever been there.

Several years earlier, in 1933, director Merian C. Cooper had come up with a variation of this process and called it miniature projection. You may not recognize the name of this technique but the result is undoubtedly familiar: King Kong. The most popular movie monster of all was actually an eighteen-inch rubber model covered in dyed rabbits' fur. The only full-scale sections of Kong were a bearhide-covered head and shoulders and a giant mechanical arm used to grab Kong's screaming girlfriend through an apartment window.

To make the miniature ape appear twenty times the size of actress Fay Wray, Cooper and special effects wizard Willis O'Brien devised a unique method which involved photographing the actress first, then projecting this footage onto a small rear screen. In front of this was placed Kong, who now seemed as large as he was supposed to be. Next, each frame of the live action was stopped as animators brought the giant ape's movements in line with Miss Wray's and photographed the two of them together.

In the famous scene where Kong yanks at her clothing, Cooper describes how this was done: "A movie was first taken of her alone while invisible wires pulled off her clothes. Then the miniature Kong was placed on a set built on a waisthigh platform, about twice the size of a dining-room table, on which miniature trees, ferns and plaster-of-paris rocks had been arranged. Back of this the movie of Fay Wray was projected, and Kong's movements made to correspond with it."

After the box-office success of King Kong, movie studios began churning out monster movies. Most were cheap imitations, but one stands out because it featured a memorable character who appeared in almost every sequence, but who was not seen until the end of the movie.

Based on a book by H. G. Wells, the movie, *The Invisible Man* (1940), concerns a brilliant scientist who discovers a formula to make himself invisible. Unfortunately, it also drives him mad. He proceeds to run around nude, derail trains, rob banks and murder people.

The scenes in which he remained totally invisible were relatively simple to arrange by using wires to move the objects he was supposedly handling. Scenes in which he was partially clothed in a topcoat, proved to be more of a problem, since wires couldn't simulate a natural drape and movement.

Borrowing techniques from stage magicians, special effects man John P. Fulton came up with a solution. A stunt man was dressed from head to foot in a black velvet costume, complete with gloves and mask. Over this he put on the invisible man's clothing and went through the motions of the scene against a matching black velvet background. In the laboratory, the film of the spooky clothing, moving across a dead black field was matted into a previously filmed background, resulting in an unusually effective illusion.

Because of the lack of air circulation inside the suit, the work was difficult and took its toll on the stuntman, who fainted twice from the heat despite the air tubes that ran up the legs of his tights and enabled him to breathe. Endless retakes were necessary before the stunt-man learned to move naturally. "We had to rehearse and rehearse," Fulton later recalled. "We made many takes. As a rule, by 'Take 20' of any such scene, we felt ourselves merely well-started toward getting our shot." Even so, the eye slits of the stuntman's mask were plain-ly visible in the finished print, making it necessary for a team of retouch artists to paint them out on 64,000 frames of film!

At the end of *The Invisible Man* when the mortally wounded madman loses his invisibility, Fulton pro-vided a particularly chilling bit of trickery. First, all we can see looking down on the death bed is a depression in the pillow and a sheet draped over the invisible form. Gradually, the bones of the "Invisible Man" ap-pear and are fleshed out by muscles, nerves and, finally, skin.

This striking sequence was done by the camera with no matte work involved. The pillow and sheet were made of plaster and papier-mâché, and the rest was Fulton's sophisticated reverse version of Méliès' old illusion: In a series of "stop motion" shots, a skeleton was dissolved into a more complete dummy and so forth, ending with actor Claude Rains.

Tapped by Cecil B. DeMille to recreate God's work in the Biblical epic, *The Ten Commandments* (1956), Fulton obliged the master director by creating screen miracles never before attempted. Of the many outstand-ing effects in the film, Fulton's most spectacular was the parting of the Red Sea, when the Israelites escaped from pursuing Egyptian soldiers. Rated as the most expensive and difficult single special effect ever produced, the scene cost nearly $500,000, and the filming and lab work took a total of six months.

Exterior scenes were shot on location on the banks of the Red Sea and the remainder was filmed in Hollywood. The parting of the sea was accomplished by the construction of a 360,000-gallon tank and waterfall that took up so much room the fence between the Paramount and RKO lots had to be torn down to provide space for it.

The waterfall was filmed several times from different angles, including mirror shots which placed the waterfall on the opposite side of the frame. Technicians combined the facing waterfalls on one strip of film, slowed it down and ran it backwards; this gave the illusion of huge walls of water pulling up and away. Pursuing Egyptian soldiers and fleeing Israelites were matted in, as was the sky and an opposing wall of water on the other bank. To close the sea, which engulfs the soldiers, the composite film was run forward so that two waterfalls seemed to be meeting and filling in the gap with water. A quick cut was made to a full body of water before the dividing line became apparent. In all, as many as twelve shots were incorporated into one frame of film.

For years *The Ten Commandments* stood as the ultimate special effects picture, until Stanley Kubrick released *2001: A Space Odyssey* in 1968. Spending more than $10,000,000 on top technicians and materials, Kubrick produced a visual tour de force in which special effects became the most important element of the movie.

Summing up the power of the film, critic John Brosnan wrote that *"2001* created such a vivid and unforgettable impression of man in space that the actual moon landing, which took place the following year after the picture's release, seemed an anticlimax."

An exacting movie magician, Kubrick utilized practically every known movie effect and, when nothing else would do the trick, he invented some new ones. The docking of a spaceship to an earth-orbiting space station, for instance, was accomplished by intricately combining half a dozen tried-and-true elements.

First, miniatures of the ship and space station were animated separately against a black velvet backdrop. Moving the miniatures a frame at a time gave the illusion of the spaceship floating toward the revolving space station. Next, they were matted into a film of a painting of the moon and earth and the black outer space between them. Then, just as the spaceship was about to land, Kubrick cut to a full-sized set of the inside of the ship and rear-projected close-up footage of the miniature space station onto the window of the cockpit, in front of the actors.

Modern engineering principles also figured in the making of *2001*. Astronaut Gary Lockwood appeared to be jogging effortlessly around the inside of a giant thirty-eight-foot centrifuge that supposedly provided gravity for the Jupiter-bound crew, but in reality he and the camera stayed in place. The wheel moved.

For the "mind-storm" sequence just before the spaceship passes through the gates of time, chemists' slides the size of this book were photographed with high-powered magnifying lenses, then blown up on the large screen. Those magnificent starbursts and nebular explosions were actually drops of dye squeezed between the glass and photographed in slow motion.

Of Kubrick's many innovations, his most important is undoubtedly the front-projection process, which was quickly adopted by the film industry. Sharper and

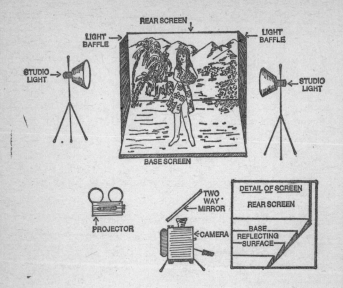

clearer than rear projection, the new process made it virtually impossible to detect any difference between the live action and the background.

To achieve the illusion of actors dressed as apes menaced by a growling leopard on an African desert, for example, Kubrick called into play that old magician's standby, the mirror. In MGM's London studio, a two-way "see through" mirror was positioned at a forty-five degree angle between the camera and a beaded screen that reflected light in an optically perfect straight line. The actors emoted in front of the screen while a projector threw the African background—including the leopard—onto the reflecting part of the mirror. The image was bounced to the screen and back again to the camera, this time with the actors included.

Nineteen sixty-eight was also the year of *Bonnie and Clyde,* a film especially popular with movie-goers who wanted their screen illusions conjured up in the form of blood-and-guts violence. As usual, special effects magicians rose to the challenge and injected new life into the gangster movie. In fact, the dream-like death scene of the outlaw couple was so successful that it started a fad of actors dying in slow motion while being riddled with bullets.

The bullet shots, looking agonizingly real as they blew holes into the bodies of Warren Beatty and Faye Dunaway, were actually tiny gelatin bags filled with red liquid and charged with gunpowder. Dozens of these "squibs" were mounted on thin steel plates backed with foam rubber and concealed under the actors' clothing. A similar procedure was followed for their vintage yellow Ford. Holes were drilled in the body, filled with explosive charges, plugged up and painted over. At just the right moment director Arthur Penn pushed a button and detonated the squibs, producing a technicolor bloodbath of squirming bodies in the throes of death.

By 1973 movie-goers were ready for the grotesqueries offered by *The Exorcist,* the story of a thirteen-year-old girl possessed by the Devil. Many of the effects were truly remarkable, not the least of which was the gruesome transformation of actress Linda Blair.

"We had to turn this sweet little girl into something pretty loathsome," explains make-up artist Dick Smith, whose idol is Jack Pierce, creator of Boris Karloff's Frankenstein make-up. "To cover her with swollen, scabby, pus-filled cuts, we used molds of baked latex. We placed the cuts very carefully, in such a way as to make her face look as lopsided as possible. We took off the eyebrows for a hideous skull-like look of *The*

Phantom of the Opera, the Lon Chaney version. It's about as evil as you can get with a little girl, I think."

Most ingenious of all was the vomiting device Smith fitted over Linda's mouth. To get her to throw up for each take, Smith designed an apparatus with two flat plastic tubes buried inside a latex half-mask glued onto Linda's jaw. The tubes ran down her back into a bag full of warm pea soup and, on cue, an electric pump spewed the soup into the actress' mouth, to be spit back out again.

After the unprecedented success of *The Exorcist,* Hollywood magicians set to work scaring people in a series of disaster pictures. In *The Towering Inferno,* occupants of a super-high skyscraper were burned to death by matting them into footage of a miniature building with butane flames leaping out of the windows. And passengers of a jumbo jet in *Airport 75* narrowly avoided a crash after their plane collided with another in mid-air, also thanks to miniatures.

By far, the most creative job of destruction by movie magicians is to be seen in *Earthquake* (1975). Veteran craftsmen Clifford Stine and Al Whitlock took on the formidable task of destroying contemporary Los Angeles by first constructing miniature duplicates of all the important buildings in the city. Exteriors were filmed at some of the actual buildings with the actors pretending to be caught in a major earthquake. Later, the miniatures were vibrated apart at pre-cut stress points while being filmed in fast motion which, when projected at normal speed, made the falling wood and styrofoam appear to be as heavy as steel and concrete. These key elements were later matted together by hand to produce spectacular vistas of a devastated city.

In one especially breathtaking scene, an office building seems to buckle under the impact of the tremors.

The illusion was achieved by a remarkably simple device thought up by director Mark Robson. No manipulation of camera or film was involved. The building was photographed in a reflecting plastic mirror, bent by hand to produce the desired effect.

Striving for complete realism when shooting scenes inside the buildings, Robson devised a rocker platform on which such key sets as a bedroom, a bar and an office were constructed. The platform was mounted on springs attached to hydraulic rams and electric motors, enabling Robson to vary the intensity of the tremors.

To heighten the effect of the earthquake, Universal Studios added an extra soundtrack to the picture, consisting of loud, low-frequency electronic sounds in the 16-to-20-cycle range. Since sound at that level is felt rather than heard, the device was genuinely frightening. Ballyhooed as "Sensurround," the vibrations had one disadvantage: it set off burglar alarms in nearby shops—and the studio was forced to drop it from screenings at small theaters.

The gimmick was reminiscent of others used for previous movies. For *The Tingler,* a Vincent Price horror picture, theater seats were wired to shock the customers into *feeling* horror. *Scent of Mystery* tried to play tricks on noses by wafting through the theater fifty artificial scents ranging from garlic to shoe polish. Unfortunately, "Glorious Smell-o-Vision" signed its own death warrant by advertising with the following slogan: "First They Moved (1893)—Then They Talked (1927)—Now They Smell (1959)."

Smaller in scale than *Earthquake,* the movie version of the best-selling book, *Jaws* (1975), was as difficult to film, but for different reasons. "The film was a nightmare and presented all sorts of problems," explains director Steve Spielberg, "one of which was the fact that we had to film most of it in splashing water."

Rather than use an animated miniature of the white shark floating in a studio tank, the producers of *Jaws* decided to construct a life-sized replica of the man-eater. Veteran special effects man Bob Mattey—who won an Academy Award for his giant mechanical squid in Walt Disney's *20,000 Leagues Under the Sea* (1954) —obliged by constructing a twenty-five-foot-long robot-fish that was able to jump out of the water, smash a boat and "eat" people.

Nicknamed "Bruce" by cast and crew, the fierce-looking plastic shark was actually three models so that it could be filmed from all angles: one with machinery exposed on the left side; one with machinery exposed on the right side; and a full shark that could be pulled behind a boat as if the shark were in hot pursuit. Mattey could make the first two swim, jump and eat by a complicated network of twenty-five remote-controlled valves and twenty electric and pneumatic hoses. Backbones of the beasts were made of spring steel.

Despite such complicated equipment, the sharks proved difficult to control during filming in the Atlantic Ocean off Martha's Vineyard. Occasionally the sharks would fail to operate and start to drift off to sea. One "Bruce" even managed to sink one of the boats and swamp several of the actors by jumping before its cue, necessitating an emergency nose job before he was able to perform again.

Similar problems plagued the filming of *The Hindenburg* (1975), the movie recreation of a Nazi dirigible that crashed and burned in New Jersey in 1937.

Designed by *Earthquake*'s Clifford Stine, the famous German airship was constructed in three versions: a fifty-foot miniature used for long shots, a full-scale reproduction moored on the studio's back lot, and several sound-stage sets of the balloon's cabins and interior framework. Keeping the full-sized Hindenburg lashed to its landing port was a continual problem throughout filming, for even minor gusts of wind threatened to pull the craft back into its former position as "Queen of the Skies."

During the crash sequence—which Stine combined with the original footage of the disaster, painstakingly matching the movements of his stunt men with those of the real victims frame by frame—the huge blimp started to drift away from its mooring with a full complement of special effects men. Paying tribute to these legions of nearly anonymous screen magicians, actor George C. Scott grabbed for the lines and shouted, "Save them! They're the real stars of the picture."

Chapter Six

HOW EASILY CAN YOUR SENSES BE FOOLED?

Most of us place absolute trust in the evidence of our senses, which usually give us a remarkably reliable picture of the world around us. Magicians know that our perception is not as foolproof as we would like to believe, however, and they make skillful use of certain quirks and tendencies of the mind to confound and amaze us.

Suppose that as you read this page you are stretched out in a comfortable chair and sipping on an orange drink while the radio plays soft music in the background. A car door slams, followed by faint voices from the direction of the house next door. A loud roar causes you to look to a window where you see tiny red and white lights flickering in the darkness. Before turning away, you notice how large the moon looks hovering over distant rooftops.

Like a super-powerful miniature computer, your brain shifts into high gear. Within a split-second what you have tasted, seen and heard is integrated, abstracted, compared, tested and sorted to generate the appropriate response. Without this ability to filter and decode data fed into the brain by the senses, you would be adrift in a sea of random, meaningless sensations.

Past experience stored in your brain as memory tells you that your neighbors usually arrive home at this hour and that a jet airplane is coming in for landing at a nearby airport. Satisfied that what you have perceived is accurate, you take another sip of soda, try to tune out a commercial on the radio, and continue reading.

But wait a minute!

Can you be absolutely certain the noise and voices coming from outside were not those of burglars there to ransack the neighbor's house? And how do you know that the engine roar and lights flickering in the night did not belong to a flying saucer? As unlikely as these hypotheses may be, they cannot be completely ruled out, for you are relying on visual and aural clues which you associate with past experience. And believe it or not, you have already been fooled by two familiar objects:

The orange-flavored soft drink contains no orange. It is a compound of colored chemicals designed to trick your taste buds. The moon has not altered its size or moved closer to earth. Orbiting near the horizon where it is on a scale with buildings and houses, the moon looks much larger than it does alone in the sky. Moreover, the radio station has tricked you into listening to a catchy advertising jingle by slightly raising the volume.

Our customary ways of perceiving the world enables the magician to trick our senses, too.

Herrmann's bird-cage disappearance, for instance, was effective (see page 19) because the spectator believed the cage to be rigid like the ones he had seen elsewhere. He hadn't a clue that it actually collapsed—especially since it contained an apparently live canary.

The more natural looking the prop, the more effective the deception is. A hat is most often used for pro-

116

ductions because it is more familiar than elaborate tubes and boxes would be. It arouses less suspicion. The cut-and-restored rope may have an end disguised to look like the middle, but to the audience it looks like a rope anyone might purchase in a hardware store.

Often our expectations are so strong that they trigger the imagination and sweep us along, even though we know what appears to be happening is not possible. When a woman is sawed in half, shreds of cloth flying through the air and the buzz of the blade sawing through flesh and bone causes us to wince. The simulation is so powerful that many people can almost feel the blade and have to close their eyes to shut out the image.

The association between cause and effect is the basis of sleight-of-hand, which Doug Henning claims "should be known as sleight of mind." A hand making a tossing motion suggests an image of the coin the magician showed to the audience a moment ago. The coin, of course, is concealed in the palm of his other hand, which we never suspect because the hand is open. We are used to seeing a fist closed—when there is an object held in the palm. Often the sequence of cause and effect is already accomplished by the time the intent of the trick is announced. And we can't see how the magician has fooled us.

Equally important to the conjurer in his battle of matching wits with the audience, is our limited attention span. Normally, we can watch only one thing at a time taking place onstage. Blackstone Sr. took advantage of this "point of focus," and during each performance, one of his assistants would "accidentally" trip while leaving the stage. This distraction gave Blackstone enough time to grab a load of silks for his hat. Whenever a fishbowl was brought onstage for a vanish,

117

Thurston would make sure that it was filled to the brim so that everyone would be watching to see whether the pretty girl assistant would spill water on her velvet evening gown. As magic scholar Henry Hay points out, "The loudest noise, the fastest motion, the brightest color will capture the attention."

The ease with which a skillful magician can fool our senses should make us question our powers of observation. Psychologists who study the quirks of the mind and senses that result in illusions tell us there are two kinds of perception: *objective reality*—the way things really are—and *phenomenal reality*—the way things appear to be. Because our perceptual systems are usually so reliable and work almost automatically, we believe we experience only objective reality, the same as everyone else.

To find how faulty this concept is, play a round of the game of Gossip. Write down a sentence, something funny but with meaning, such as: "The football coach is bouncing on a birthday cake in the chemistry lab." Whisper the words to the person next to you and have him or her pass the message down the line. The last one to hear it repeats the sentence out loud, and everyone will be amazed to hear the result. It may turn out to be: "The chemistry teacher baked a football cake and tossed it into the gym."

The flaw in memory accounts for the conflicting testimony of witnesses to an automobile accident. When we hear a screech of tires and a crash, then turn to see the wrecked cars, there is an unconscious tendency to reconstruct the events leading to the accident and to later remember that we saw it. "He lies like an eyewitness," goes on old German saying.

Often, what we perceive is not what is there, despite our certainty that it is. You are no doubt positive that

118

you can tell the difference between hot and cold. If you think so, try this classic experiment devised by John Locke, the English philosopher, in 1690.

Put one hand in a bowl of hot water and the other in cold water. Wait a few minutes, then put them both into a bowl filled with lukewarm water. One hand will feel cold and the other will feel hot. How can this be? The property of hot or cold certainly resides in the water, does it not? Is your sense of touch lying to you?

While our sense of touch is rarely the focal point of a magician's trick, a vagary in our sense of hearing is often called into play to complete a magic effect. Ventriloquism is possible because our ears are limited to telling us only whether a sound is coming from the right or the left. By varying the pitch and volume of his voice, a magician can convince us that he is locked inside a box suspended over the stage, when all the while he is waiting nearby to make a mysterious reappearance.

But vision is our primary sense and, with the exception of certain mentalist effects, all magic is visual. While it might be hard to believe, vision is one of the easiest senses to fool. Look at this sketch of a magnet. Does it make sense to you? The sketch manages to short-circuit the computer of your brain, for no matter how hard your mind tries to make sense of this drawing, there is no solution. It is an impossible figure that can exist only on paper in two dimensions.

Most of what we perceive is related to a background and seen from a point of view of perspective. Light objects stand out from dark backgrounds, as well as the converse. Designers of highway signs utilize this principle to ensure safety, and magicians use it to safeguard their secret apparatus. Levitation wires painted

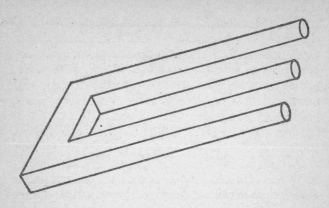

matte black to blend in with the curtains, and black wells in tables are the magician's stock in trade.

Painters, theatrical set designers, movie and television special effects men all play tricks with perspective to give the illusion of depth and dimension. Magicians construct cabinets and boxes with ingenious angles designed to make them appear to be too small for a person to be hiding inside. Houdini made perhaps the grandest use of perspective when he managed to convince an audience of thousands at New York's immense Hippodrome theater that he had vanished a five-ton elephant named Jennie from the stage.

The gentle pachyderm lumbered up a ramp into a box the size of a one-car garage which seemed too small to hold it. The curtains were drawn, Houdini fired a pistol, and when the curtains were reopened the huge cabinet was empty. Escaping through the other end was not possible without the audience seeing it. But all the while, Jennie was patiently cooling her enormous heels behind a fake panel at the side. The perspective was constructed so cleverly that the abrupt slant was not apparent from the auditorium.

Forcing is another psychological technique the magician has at his command to fool us. Partly based on educated guesswork, partly on suggestion, forcing is most often used by mentalists and card sharps. When asked to pick a number from one to ten, people will pick seven more often than any other number; from ten to twenty, the number is most often 15.

If you write the letter A, B and C on a piece of paper and ask a volunteer to choose one, he will most often pick B, or the middle object of whatever the sequence may be. A card sharp knows that if he asks a member of the audience to call out a card, the result will most often be the ace of hearts. But more than that, a good card manipulator can stack the deck and deal whatever card you ask for, seemingly off the top. In addition, he can "force" a card into your hand by watching your face and gestures to know when you are ready to choose, while you believe you have made a free choice.

By now you undoubtedly realize that the old adage of "the hand is quicker than the eye" is not true. The eye can follow the most rapid finger-work and penetrate the magician's secret—if he is not clever enough to distract the spectator's eye and brain. It is all there to see if you know where to look. But most enjoyment comes from allowing the magician to take you on whatever impossible flights he will. As Doug Henning points out, "The real magic takes place in your mind, not on the stage."

Chapter Seven

ILLUSIONS TO ASTOUND
YOUR FRIENDS

Now that we have turned the magician's bag of tricks inside out and discovered how we are deceived into believing we have witnessed the impossible, it is time to don the black silk hat ourselves and have some fun fooling others. Instructions follow for a variety of tricks, most of which can be performed almost anywhere using everyday objects.

Keep in mind that even though you know the secret, the trick won't become an illusion unless you can convince spectators that what they thought they saw actually happened. Magic is more than the simple execution of a trick.

Professionals deceive the audience with off-the-cuff talk called "patter," which provides an entertaining story line and prevents the execution of the trick from becoming dull and mechanical.

Patter also sets up misleading clues that confuse the spectator's sense of logic. While telling him you are doing one thing, in reality your hands are doing something quite different. Follow the suggestions given and rehearse your patter before beginning a trick.

As we learned in the last chapter, the secret move does not have to be invisible in every trick. You misdirect the spectator by drawing his attention elsewhere to fool his senses. Conceal an object with one hand and move the other, and your audience will look at the moving hand, for people always react to the boldest movements.

Above all, be natural and relaxed. Spooky seriousness won't work unless you possess the face and charisma of a Herrmann. Follow the example of Doug Henning, magic's newest super-wizard, and be yourself. The most successful amateur magicians, including actors Cary Grant and James Stewart and rock star Alice Cooper, adapt their tricks to suit their personalities.

Before you begin, keep in mind the three "no-nos" of wizardry:

1. NEVER PRACTICE IN PUBLIC. You will give away the secret even before you perform it.

2. NEVER REPEAT A TRICK. Go on to the next one before the audience can figure out how it was done.

3. NEVER REVEAL A SECRET. You will destroy the mystery—and the fun. If anyone insists, just say, "I'm sorry but we magicians are sworn to secrecy. It's part of the professional code." It may sound pretentious, but it usually works, especially after you have thoroughly mystified the audience.

Super Easy Tricks

Let's warm up with these never-fail bafflers which can be performed within minutes of reading the instructions, although a little practice is a good idea.

THE FRANKENSTEIN THUMB

The illusion: You remove and restore your left thumb.
The secret: (1) Bend both thumbs and bring them together. (2) Cover the thumb joints with the first two

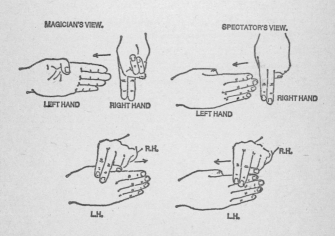

ARROWS ARE THERE TO INDICATE MOVEMENT OF HAND

fingers of your right hand. (3) Yank away your right thumb, which appears to be the first joint of your left one.

The patter: Ask those present if they know that you have had a thumb transplant: "It makes me feel a little like the Frankenstein monster." When they scoff, offer to prove it, meanwhile having prepared your hands in your lap or under a table. "Yank off" the thumb with a loud grunt as quickly as possible, for it is the element of surprise that makes this trick effective. Then, while they are still startled, apologize and "slip" it back on.

LOOSE CHANGE

Balance two or three quarters on your arm, then toss them into the air and effortlessly catch them with the same hand.

The secret: (1) Balance the coins on your arm just above the elbow. (2) Throw your arm forward while simultaneously *bending* your knees. Catch the coins.

The patter: This little display of physical agility works best as a challenge. After doing it dare an onlooker to try. He won't be able to unless he bends his knees while catching the coins.

THE GHOST PENNY

The illusion: A third penny is created from two real ones.

The secret: (1) Place two pennies together between the tips of your index fingers. Rub them together rapidly in an up-and-down movement and (2) a third "ghost" penny will seem to appear between them.

The patter: Make this optical illusion entertaining and build suspense by betting your family or friends that you can turn two coins into three.

THE MAGIC BALLOON

The illusion: A balloon changes color before the spectators' eyes.

The secret: (1) Put a blue balloon inside a red one. (2) Inflate them and an air pocket will form between the balloon walls. (3) Burst the outside balloon with a concealed tack attached to your thumb with chewing gum or wax.

The patter: Allow the purpose of the trick to sink in by asking those present to indicate which color they would like to see the red balloon turn into. When someone says, "Blue," comment on what a pretty color that is, make a few passes over the balloon and tap it directly on top. Move your hand quickly to conceal the piece of red balloon that will remain around the stem.

SIXTH SENSE

The illusion: You locate an object hidden in a room without speaking to those present.

The secret: A confederate who is present when the object is hidden signals the information to you by means of a silent code.

With your confederate, mentally divide the room to be used into four imaginary squares numbered according to the diagram below. Further divide each square into four smaller squares. Be careful to remember

127

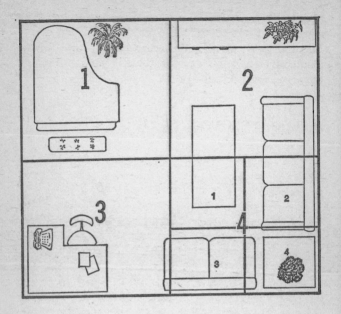

which part of the room is "up" and that the numbers run from left to right.

After the object is hidden and you enter the room, casually glance at your accomplice who will be clasping his or her hands together and gripping one or more fingers to tell you which section to look in. If the person has the fingers of his right hand curled around three of his left fingers, for instance, you will know to look in the lower left square of the room. When you have narrowed the search to a corner of the smaller square, via your confederate's second signal, a little guesswork will tell you where the object is hidden.

The patter: Announce to your audience that you have discovered that you possess a sixth sense, "something akin to Uri Geller's." After you read your accomplice's signal, don't immediately "discover" the hidden object. Make a show of it by pressing your hands to your temples as if to summon up psychic powers and gradually move toward your quarry.

MATTER THROUGH MATTER

The illusion: You slam a glass of water through a solid tabletop.

The secret: (1) Cover a glass, about one-third filled with liquid, with a doubled sheet of newspaper and shape it carefully around the glass. Lift the paper with your left hand to show that the glass is under it, and while putting it back, slip the glass (in your right hand) under the table and put it between your knees. (2) Move the shaped paper up and down while you bump the glass under the table to make it sound as if the glass is inside the paper. (3) Announce your intent and slam your fist against the paper. At the same time, act as if you're catching the glass with the other hand underneath and put the glass on the table.

The misdirection: Disguise your camouflage by stating: "Since matter can only penetrate matter in complete darkness, I will have to cover the glass." Be sure to use newspaper because it is flexible yet firm enough to conform to the shape of the glass. You direct your audience's attention away from your secret move with the newspaper lift.

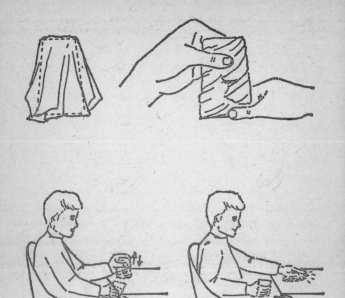

HOUDINI'S ESCAPE RING

The effect: A ring escapes from a loop of string without cutting it.

The secret: (1) Thread a loop of string through a ring and ask a spectator to volunteer his fingers to serve as poles. (2) With your left index finger loop the far side of the string over the top of the near one. (3) Pull the near string over the left pole with your right hand

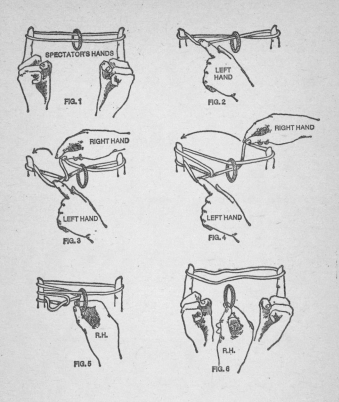

and continue holding the loop with your left. (4) Pull another loop over the left pole from the other side of the ring. (5) Finally, take the ring in your right hand and let go of the loop with your left. Pull gently on the ring and it will slide off.

Misdirection: Actually, there is no trickery involved; you just have a little more knowledge than your audience. Make this geometric trick entertaining by devising a patter about how you were rummaging in an old junk shop and the owner sold you a ring that he claimed belonged to Houdini. It can escape from strings. Say, "Sure I was as skeptical as you are—until the old man proved it to me," which you promptly do for your audience.

I'VE GOT YOUR NUMBER or MATHEMAGIC

The illusion: You correctly predict the total of a column of random numbers.

The secret: Ask someone to write down the year he was born. (A) Beneath that tell him to add the year of some important event in his life. (B) Next, have him add his age this year. (C) Now ask him to take some coins from his pocket and lay them on the table and to add the number of coins (not the amount). (D) Conclude with the number of years that have passed since the important event mentioned above. (E) Ask him to total the figures, but before he does say that you will correctly predict the number. Sure enough, you can!

(A) and (C) always add up to the current year, as do (B) and (E). Therefore, all four figures add up to double the current year—3952 in 1976—which you know in advance. The only figure you have to add is the total number of coins before you divulge the total.

The misdirection: None is needed—the subject is too busy writing and adding to think out the simple solution.

FRUIT INTO VEGETABLE

The illusion: A grape turns into a radish inside your closed hand.

The secret: Conceal a radish in your left hand before

you begin your patter and rest the hand lightly on the edge of the table. Pull a grape from a bunch with your right hand. Move it toward your left, which you simultaneously raise a few inches. (1) Drop the grape into your lap during the movement. (2) Pretend to deposit the grape into your left hand. (3) Clench your fist around the radish and point to it, which shows that the right hand is empty. Produce the radish.

The misdirection: Start talking as you reach for the grape. Bounce it in your hand and say, "You know it may be true that you can't turn a sow's ear into a silk purse, but it is possible to turn a grape into a radish." By raising your left hand and moving your right toward it, you are drawing attention to your left. This is the same technique used by stage directors to focus attention in a play.

Note: You can substitute any number of small objects for this trick: for instance, a cracker and a potato chip, a ring and a piece of metal.

Finger Magic

Sleight of hand is one of the magician's most valuable tools. Although mastering secret finger moves in the tricks which follow takes time and effort, the results are more than rewarding. You will be as delighted as your audience when you can pluck coins and small objects from their sleeves, collars—and even their ears!

With practice the muscles of your hands will loosen and you will soon develop the necessary digital skills. Start with your right hand if you are right-handed and then work on your left, or vice versa if you are left-handed. Magician-writer Henry Hay calls any conjurer who limits finger magic to one hand "a magical illiterate."

You must learn to manipulate by feel so that you do not direct attention to the hand with the coin. Compare yourself to a piano player who would detract from his performance if he watched his hands moving across the keyboard. Teach yourself the way Houdini did, by practicing in front of a mirror until the moves look natural to you.

SUPER-COOL COIN ROLL

This is not so much a trick as a flashy bit of finger-work and an excellent way to limber up the muscles of the hand for other sleights. Remember to use nothing smaller than a quarter or it will be impossible to do. Here's how actor Paul Newman does the Super-Cool Coin Roll in his tough-guy roles.

Moisten your middle knuckles with your tongue to keep the coin from slipping. (1) Hold the coin on the side of your thumb. (2) Carefully flip it onto your index finger into the fork of your knuckle and lever it onto the middle finger. (3) Do the same with your third finger. (4) When the coin reaches your pinky, roll it back across and keep going until your hand tires.

THE FAMOUS FRENCH DROP

This is one of the most famous methods of palming a coin, making it vanish and reappear anywhere you desire.

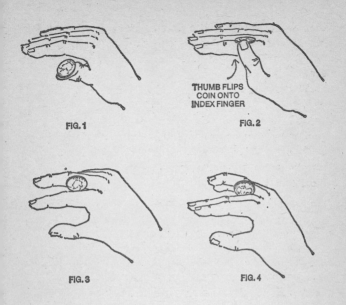

FIG. 1

THUMB FLIPS
COIN ONTO
INDEX FINGER

FIG. 2

FIG. 3

FIG. 4

The secret: (1) Hold a coin by the edges between the thumb, index and middle fingers of your left hand. (2) Reach the thumb of your right hand under the coin and your fingers over it as if you are going to grab the coin. (3) Release the coin and let it drop into the palm of your left hand and simultaneously pretend to grab it with your right. Palm it in your left, point your index finger at your clenched right fist, and with a flourish show that the hand is empty. The coin has disappeared! Note: you should hide the coin in your left hand in the two large muscle pads that form a "V"—one at the base of the thumb, the other at the heel of your hand.

The misdirection: The receiving (right) hand acts as a screen for the sleight going on behind it. Direct attention away from the palming (left) hand by clenching your right fist as if the coin were truly inside it. For the climax ask a spectator, "Please tap my hand because I need your psychic energy to make the coin disappear." Open your fingers with a flourish and wonder where the coin might have gone. Say, "Oh, there is it," and reach your left hand to someone's ear and pull it out.

Now, let's put this sleight to use in the following effect.

MILLIONAIRE'S BUCKET

The illusion: Coins caught in mid-air and odd places fill a metal bucket.

The secret: Prepare in advance a small metal bucket as shown below. Grab a palmed coin from the air. Hit

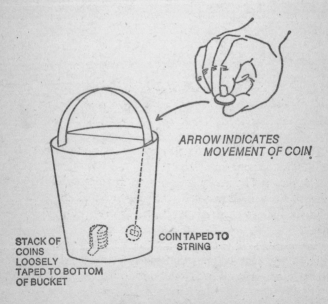

ARROW INDICATES
MOVEMENT OF COIN

STACK OF
COINS
LOOSELY
TAPED TO BOTTOM
OF BUCKET

COIN TAPED TO
STRING

the black thread across the pail with your hand as you appear to deposit the coin, causing the taped coin at the bottom of the pan to jingle. Re-palm the coin while your hand is inside the pail and continue grabbing coins in the air until you seem to have thrown in ten of them.

The misdirection: Look into the air and ask your audience if they see what you see. As they follow your glance dart your hand up and produce the palmed coin. Walk through the audience if you are a skilled coin manipulator (Robert-Houdin could palm seven at a time) and say, "Ah, there's another one!" Pull coins from ears, sleeves, trouser cuffs, and so on. Go back to the pail. After five more catches shake the taped coins loose and shake a little harder each time you throw in another one. Make up a patter along the lines of, "I hear this is how millionaires make their money."

Playing Card Magic

THE GLIDE

The illusion: You produce the ace of hearts from any position in the pack.

The secret: The ace of hearts is on the bottom of the pack where it is drawn back into the palm of the left hand so that the cards above it can be drawn one at a time.

Ask someone in your audience to give you a number, any number, then tell them that you will produce the ace of hearts, counting off to that number from the bottom of

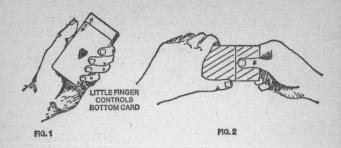

LITTLE FINGER
CONTROLS
BOTTOM CARD

FIG. 1   FIG. 2

the deck. (2) (Remember your "angles" and hold the deck down so that no one will see your secret.)

The misdirection: Hesitate for a moment before producing the ace at the appropriate number and smile nervously as if you are not sure the trick will work. This will give you a second to push the ace forward with the little finger of your left hand, and will prevent you from pulling out the wrong card with your right.

THE FORCE

The illusion: A spectator freely selects a playing card which you promptly identify.

The secret: Hold a deck of cards in your left hand (1) with your little finger stuck inside holding the break above the "force" card, whose identity you already know. Riffle the deck with your right hand until the volunteer says, "Stop!" Ignore the riffle cut, lift the packet, show the card (2), and identify it.

The misdirection: Holding the cards comfortably with your little finger stuck inside takes practice. Keep talking and riffling the cards in front of the volunteer so that he doesn't get a chance to see what you are really doing. Keep asking him, "Are you absolutely certain that I am not using mental powers to force you to select the eight of spades?" Then prove you are doing just that. If you are skillful enough he won't realize that the break was not the one he made.

PICK A CARD!

The illusion: A card freely selected by a volunteer turns up in the deck at just the position you said it would.

The secret: Before starting, stack the bottom of the deck with a six of clubs turned face up, followed by five cards face down. Riffle the deck and allow the spectator to select any card and then to place it on top of the pack.

Place the cards on a table and ask the person to cut the deck and put the two piles together. Snap your fingers over the cards, then spread them out. Your indicator card will now be exposed and the volunteer will quickly tell you that it was not the card chosen.

Remove the cards above the six of clubs and ask the volunteer to count back the number of places on the indicator card. Sure enough, the card the person selected is six places back.

Misdirection: Be careful not to riffle the cards too openly while the spectator is choosing or you will reveal the face-up card. Make up a patter along the lines of, "Here's a deck of cards with a mind of its own. It does its own tricks."

Books and Magic Clubs

For those of you who wish to go on to more complicated tricks, the following books are recommended:

Gibson, Walter, *Professional Magic for Amateurs*
Hay, Henry, *The Amateur Magician's Handbook*
Kaye, Marvin, *The Stein and Day Handbook of Magic*
Scarne, John, *Scarne on Card Tricks, Scarne's Magic Tricks*
Severn, Bill, *Bill Severn's Big Book of Magic*

Amateurs are welcome to join professionals in the Society of American Magicians (S.A.M.) and the International Brotherhood of Magicians (I.B.M.). Membership entitles you to attend meetings that feature programs and films on new and old magic effects, as well as to receive their magazines. For more information, write:

The Society of American Magicians
66 Marked Tree Road
Needham, Massachusetts 02192

The International Brotherhood of Magicians
Kenton, Ohio
(No Street address necessary)

Chapter Eight

DEVELOPING A SUPER
MAGIC MEMORY

While the purpose of magic is to delight an audience, magic also offers more lasting benefits to the magician.

Learning to perform tricks can be an effective way to overcome shyness and open the doors to friendship and popularity. Therapists at such hospitals as Bellevue, the Mayo Clinic and the Sister Kenny Institute have long recognized the beneficial effect of magic on the handicapped and mentally disturbed, whose self-confidence soars dramatically when they learn to execute a few simple deceptions.

More important, there is skill useful to all that can be borrowed from magic. Used properly, it can improve your performance in school, on the job, in your social life, as well as enable you to perform amazing mental acrobatics. This especially helpful technique is called mnemonics (disregard the first "m", and it as easy to pronounce). Mnemonics is akin to the mind-reading codes of mentalists, and is the key to the mysterious skills of the once-popular magician known as a memory artist.

Memory artists were a favorite of vaudeville audiences, and the act went something like this: An assistant wheeled in a table with an adding machine while "Mr.

Memory" called for a volunteer to operate the machine and another to chalk a column of twelve four-digit numbers on a blackboard behind him.

At the assistant's signal of "Go!" Mr. Memory and the operator of his mechanical challenger turned to look at the figures on the blackboard. A few seconds later, while the machine continued to clatter noisily, Mr. Memory stepped up to the board and wrote down the correct total. A few moments later, the adding machine caught up with him and verified the sum.

Next, Mr. Memory asked the audience to call out words, any words. Trying their best to stump him, spectators called out the funniest and longest words they could think of, and his assistant wrote all of them in numbered order on the blackboard. But Mr. Memory could rarely be foiled—he immediately repeated the one hundred or so words without a single mistake. "Mummy-gum-peristeum-acacia honey-perambulator-Magyar-salmagundi-Ruthenia-theosophy - ferromanganese-pharynx-lenticular," and so on. Each word was rattled off in order, and none was missing.

Lest the audience think he could somehow see the blackboard behind him, Mr. Memory always repeated the list backwards. Adding an applause-provoking touch, he then asked the audience to call out any of the words and instantly rattled off the word's corresponding number. Finally, he requested numbers and called out the corresponding word.

Memory artists are rare today, but their once-secret techniques are being taught by a variety of memory schools and explained in books. The latest is a bestseller, *The Memory Book*, by memory experts Harry Lorayne and Jerry Lucas, the latter an ex-basketball star, who have updated several classic mnemonic systems.

Right now mnemonic feats probably sound impossible for you to do. Like most of us, you probably can commit to memory only about seven words called out in rapid succession. But by learning the following system, in which the imagination is used to stimulate the intellect, you should be able to recall instantly twenty-five words after practicing for only half an hour!

First, you must master the key list below until you can repeat the words forwards and backwards and out of sequence. This is an easier task than it might appear. Each presents a vivid picture in your mind, and each picture brings to mind its number.

1. A skyscraper.
   You visualize a solitary skyscraper, perhaps the Empire State Building, which towers over all the others. It looks like a giant number *one*.

2. A pair of jeans.
   There are *two* legs.

3. A stool.
   It has *three* legs.

4. A door.
   It has *four* corners.

5. A glove.
   It has *five* fingers.

6. A cube.
   Half a pair of dice is a *six*-sided cube. Imagine a *six* on the die.

7. A $100 bill.
   You are lucky and have won $100 from the lottery with the number *seven*, which is a lucky number.

8. A gate.
   A gate sounds like an *eight*.

9. A cat.
   A cat has *nine* lives.

10. A pair of shoes.
    There are 10 toes inside your shoes.

11. A hammock.
    The poles at each end form an *11*.

12. A sandwich.
    Twelve o'clock is lunchtime.

13. A cast on your leg.
    You had bad luck and broke your leg. *Thirteen* is an unlucky number.

14. A diploma.
    At *14* you graduate from grammar school.

15. A tennis game.
    In tennis, the first score counts *15* points.

16. An automobile.
    At *16* you are able to obtain a driver's license.

17. Playing cards.
    In the game of blackjack, the minimum "stay" score for the dealer is *17*.

18. A soldier.
    At *18* a young man can join the army.

19. A cowboy twirling a lasso.
    The cowboy is standing (the *one*) and the lasso resembles a *nine*.

20. Cigarettes.
Cigarettes come *20* to a pack.

21. A wedding.
At *21* you can marry without your parents' permission.

22. A pair of nuns.
The figure *two* resembles a hooded nun.

23. A nun and a giant frog.
The frog (the spring-shaped *three*) is leaping behind the nun as they walk together.

24. A Christmas tree.
Christmas Eve comes on the *twenty-fourth* of December.

25. Stars.
Imagine seeing five five-pointed stars in the night sky.

Don't be disturbed by the absurd images some of these key words conjure up, for this is the source of the system's power. The images must be vivid enough so that you can see them clearly in your mind's eye and not confuse one with the other.

Start by memorizing the first ten keys, remembering to associate the shape of the image with its number. Now, let's take ten nouns at random and see how easily the association technique works.

1. *Aunt Millie.* Imagine that Aunt Millie is on top of a *skyscraper,* on the observation deck or, even stronger, that she is clinging to the spire for dear life. Key number one.

2. *An ice cream cone.* You have dropped a

chocolate cone on your new *jeans* and you have to go home and change them. Key two.

3. *A buffalo*. A buffalo is balanced precariously on a small *stool*. Key three.

4. *A bicycle*. You are taking your bicycle into the living room through the front *door*. Key four.

5. *A cold*. Your nose is running, and to find your handkerchief, you must remove your *glove*. Key five.

6. *A rug*. You throw a giant pair of dice on the table and one *cube* falls onto the rug.

7. *A postcard*. You have just won *$100* in a lottery, and a postcard has informed you of your good luck.

8. *Toothpaste*. Someone has written words all over a *gate* with pink toothpaste.

9. *A hat*. You have just bought a new hat and you are annoyed to find your *cat* sleeping on it.

10. *Love*. Your girlfriend or boyfriend has bought you a new pair of green *shoes* for your birthday.

The ten examples could just as easily be associated with other key images if they were presented in different order. If a postcard were the first word, for example, you could imagine it soaring on the wind and landing on top of a skycraper. By the same token, if a buffalo were number 10, you could fantasize the animal trying to squeeze its two front hooves into a pair of your shoes. Even abstract words like love, which are more difficult to remember, can be effectively coded by

146

giving them a visual context, In this case the gift of a pair of shoes.

Mnemonics works so well because we all think in visual images. The philosopher Aristotle was one of the first to point this out in his *De Anima,* written about 300 B.C.: "Imagination is the intermediary between perception and thought . . . the mind never thinks without a mental picture. The thinking faculty thinks of its forms in pictures. No one could ever learn or understand anything if he had not the faculty of perception; even when he thinks speculatively, he must have some mental picture with which to think."

The connection between the key image and the new word must be logical and it must also be outrageous, as with the buffalo trying to perch on a stool. The two working together form a vivid scene that sticks in your memory, for the unusual stays in your mind whether it is comic, frightening, sad or ridiculous.

In visualizing these striking images, you will instantly recall each word in the list as you think of the number, a feat that will amaze you as well as your friends. This method can also be put to the practical purpose of keying the salient points of an important lecture, if for some reason you are unable to take notes.

In some cases it may be more useful to put the key images aside and construct associations based on the material itself. Perhaps you have written a speech which you have to deliver in front of the class. In trying to memorize it, you notice that you have tied the three major points to jokes which are easier to remember, as in the following:

1. A fat lady entered a drugstore and asked for reducing pills. The clerk, standing in a narrow aisle, said, "Walk this way, please," and the woman

answered, "If I could walk that way I wouldn't need the pills."

2. I asked a friend if he could define a moron and he said, "Sure. That's a guy who parts his hair in the middle and has more on one side than the other."

3. I complained to a waiter that there was a fly in my soup and he told me, "Oh, that'll be 50 cents extra for the meat."

To keep the elements of the speech in your mind, key them to the jokes and the rest will fall into place: (1) fat lady, (2) moron, and (3) fly. Imagine that a fat lady who is a moron is chasing a fly, and no matter how nervous you become, the flesh of your speech will reappear in your mind when you visualize these bare bones.

Free associations also work well for remembering long words and learning foreign languages. Mr. Memory remembered a word like salmagundi by breaking it down into parts, *salami* and *gun*. Pharynx could be recalled as *far inks*, and perambulator could be visualized as a *pear* in an *ambulance* stuck in *tar*.

Organizing numerically and alphabetically is also important to remembering. If you have to go to the supermarket and have forgotten your list, it will be a help if you can remember how many items were on it. Then you can try to remember how many were dairy items, meat items, vegetables and so forth, until you pinpoint them.

Outlining lessons is always done with numbers or letters to facilitate learning. It would be difficult to remember the list of divine prohibitions if they had not been numbered and made easier to absorb as the Ten Commandments. And the 50 United States would be almost impossible to remember if we did not list them alphabetically. Try listing the major points of a subject the next time you are studying for a test or trying to remember facts, and associate them freely or link them to the key images, and you will probably see dramatic results. But remember: *You must have thoroughly memorized the master key images or you will simply confuse yourself.*

Another method to reinforce memory makes use of verse and rhyme. Singing commercials are prime examples of how this technique can even make us remember information in which we have no interest. Many of us use this helpful technique without realizing it in rhymes such as:

> Thirty days has September
> April, June and November.

Or the helpful spelling cue:

> I before "e"
> Except after "c,"
> Or when sounded like "a,"
> As in neighbor or weigh.

Remembering names is a problem that plagues us all, but not Harry Lorayne, co-author of *The Memory Book*. During his demonstrations, Lorayne performs a Mr. Memory act by calling off the names of the 100 or so people he has met before his lecture. He never fails to name them all by using a few simple mnemonic tricks.

Perhaps you are in a new class or a new job and you want to make an impression by remembering everyone by name, a "trick" guaranteed to please. Using the master list of images, imagine Joe Lewis as a window washer on the skyscraper (No. 1) and about to fall, Sarah Tomlin wearing jeans (No. 2) so tight they hurt, and Bobbie Brooks, who may be a little overweight, sitting uncomfortably on a stool (No. 3).

Using a direct association, you can look for an image in the name itself and then associate it with a noticeable characteristic of the person to whom it belongs. Mrs. Byrd might be a thin, short woman with a high-pitched voice, whom you could think of as a robin chirping. (Don't overload yourself with similar images, however, or you may come out with "Hello, Mrs. Robin," because you have associated someone else with a different kind of a bird.) Mr. Knight may be tall and courtly; Mr. Baker may have thick fingers that you can see kneading bread dough. Miss Marvin may bring to mind no specific image, but you can remember her name by thinking of it as a marred vine. Mr. Basham can be seen bashing a ham as if it were a punching bag. Mr. Weiner could be seen wolfing down a giant hot dog.

Numbers are the most difficult to encode mnemonically because they are entirely abstract and require symbols before they can be made into words and images. To create a master key list, each number must correspond to one letter of the alphabet. Since there are only ten digits in our numerical system, we need only ten letters.

The classic system disregards the six vowels (a-e-i-o-u) as well as "y," which often is pronounced as a vowel, and translates numbers into consonant sounds, as follows:

1—d or t	6—g (soft sound) or j, ch, sh
2—n	7—g (hard sound) or k
3—m	8—t or v
4—r	9—b or p
5—l	0—soft c or s, z

Number 42 translates into "r-n," which can be encoded as the word rain, since vowels do not count and thus will not confuse the sequence. Number 916 can be translated into the word pitch, and the number 3,170,850 becomes a sentence, My dog has fleas:

```
3 1 7 0 8 5 0
m d g s f l s
```

You can keep important dates and numbers in your mind by translating them into easily remembered sentences. An appointment at 2:00 on February 14th can become "none dare." Again, once you have thoroughly committed the code to memory, you can easily recall your social security number, bank account number and important telephone numbers.

If you can convince a friend to memorize the code numbers, you will be able to perform a mind-reading stunt that is one of the Amazing Kreskin's most baffling. Tell your audience that you know someone who can read thoughts from a great distance; then ask a person in the audience to write any three-digit number on a large sheet of paper.

"Make it hard and don't repeat any number," you indicate. "Now everyone look at the number and concentrate on it." Ask a volunteer to dial your friend on the telephone and tell the person to ask for Mr. Verne. The fictitious "Mr. Verne" will immediately tell the caller that the number he or she is thinking of is 842 because that is the code for VERNE. All you have to do is quickly make up a name, not always easy if it is to sound genuine.

Requesting a volunteer not to repeat a number in succession will make it easier because that means you will not have to work with double consonants.

Perhaps this old magic "trick" will work for you as it did for Jerry Lucas, who graduated Phi Beta Kappa from Ohio State University, "having put in something like one-fourth the study time that most students used," while becoming an All-American basketball star.

Mnemonic, you will find, is a fascinating game with many practical applications.

GLOSSARY

ANGLES: The sight line of the audience in relation to the trick being performed. A constant source of worry to magicians who fear spectators will see what they have palmed or their apparatus.

ANIMATION: Making a prop such as a handkerchief, doll or puppet seem to have a life of its own. In movies, the filming of drawings, puppets and other objects so that they seem to move.

ANTICIPATION: Convincing the audience that the secret move has not yet occurred, when in reality it has. A form of misdirection.

APPARATUS: Props used for effects, as opposed to genuine, everyday objects also used by the conjurer.

ASSISTANT: person who helps the magician on stage and is identified as part of the act. Compare with confederate and plant.

BILLET: A small piece of paper used in mentalist effects.

BLACK ART: The technique of making persons and objects invisible by covering them in black velvet to match the stage background; the audience cannot delineate dead black against dead black. The motion picture matte process uses a similar technique.

BREAKAWAYS: Comedy props such as a breakaway wand which look normal in the hands of the conjurer but which break apart in the hands of a volunteer from the audience. In movies any prop that is made to fall apart at the slightest pressure, such as a balsawood chair used in a barroom fight.

CENTER TEAR: A secret move in which the magician palms the center of a billet to learn its contents while tearing it up and burning it.

CHANGING BAG: A black velvet bag mounted on a long handle that resembles a butterfly net. It is used to change one object into another by turning the handle, which opens an inside lining with a concealed object.

COLD READING: Mentalist effect which uses psychology and disguised questions to ferret out information to tell the subject amazingly accurate facts about himself.

CONFEDERATE: The magician's secret assistant who poses as an audience volunteer.

CONFUSION: Giving an audience so many details about an effect that the audience fails to see the secret move. A form of misdirection.

ESCAPES: A branch of magic in which the performer frees himself after being shackled or bound.

FLASH PAPER: Chemically treated tissue paper that ignites in a brief flash. Used to cover a quick vanish of a small object.

FOO CAN: A gimmick that fits inside a container to make it appear empty. By tilting it, the liquid inside can be poured out.

FORCE: Making the spectator select a specific card, even though he believes he is making a free choice.

FRENCH DROP: Sleight of hand that allows the magician to hold onto a coin or ball while seeming to drop it into the other hand.

GIMMICK: A secret bit of apparatus that is the key to the trick.

GUILLOTINE EFFECT: A spectator's finger is placed inside a small wooden pillory in which a sharp blade previously dropped, guillotine-fashion, and sliced through a carrot. A fake cut-out blade is substituted for the real one while drawing it back up and preparing it for the finger.

HOLDER: A device, hidden on the person of the performer, which contains handkerchiefs or other small loads.

HOULETTE: A container for a deck of cards gimmicked with a spring or thread to produce the effect of cards rising one by one.

LEGERDEMAIN: Originally a French word that means light of hand. Magicians use it to refer to the manipulation of small objects, but the public uses it to mean magic in general.

LOAD: A bag of hidden objects to be produced in an effect.

MAGICIAN'S WAX: An invisible, sticky substance often used to attach a thread to the rising cards.

MISDIRECTION: Diverting an audience's attention from a secret move or device. A cornerstone of the psychology of deception.

MUSCLE READING: A mentalist effect wherein the magician is led to a hidden object by the unconscious movements of a person trying to keep the secret.

PALMING: Sleight of hand to conceal a coin, card or other small object in the palm or another part of the hand.

PATTER: What the magician says while performing. Patter provides misdirection, pacing for the act and comedy relief.

PEEK MIRROR: A tiny mirror glued to the performer's finger or the frame of his glasses in order to see the faces of cards he is holding up to the audience, or to see what is being written or drawn while the mentalist's back is turned.

PLANT: A confederate placed in the audience to obtain information about a spectator or to rise as a volunteer.

PRESTIDIGITATION: Originally meant fast fingerwork, but now is used to refer to all kinds of magic.

PSI FACTOR: The unknown power that accounts for paranormal phenomena such as ESP.

ROUGHING FLUID: A friction-producing substance that is used to make cards adhere. Two cards can then be shown as one.

SALTING: Hiding apparatus and other objects in a room or on a stage where the magician is going to appear.

SERVANTE: A hidden receptacle in the magician's table.

SET-UP: Arranging a deck of cards so that the magician or card sharp knows exactly what he is dealing. Also known as a system.

SILK: Sheer handkerchiefs used in productions and vanishes. They are easy to conceal and when produced seem much larger than they are.

SLEIGHT OF HAND: Secret hand moves to manipulate coins and other small objects. Often referred to simply as a sleight.

SPRING FLOWERS: Fake flowers on springs that suddenly seem to bloom from their hiding place.

STEAL: To obtain secretly an object produced in the effect.

STRIPPER DECK: A deck of cards with tapered edges. When one is reversed, the magician can locate it by feel.

SUCKER EFFECT: Leading the audience to believe they have seen the magician's secret or caught him making a mistake. The real climax of the trick seems impossible.

TRANSPOSITION: A trick in which two people or objects mysteriously change places.

TRAPS: Concealed openings on the surface of the magician's table, referred to as black art wells. The black velvet openings are disguised in the design of the tabletop and are used to dispose of props and gimmicks.

VANISH: To make an object or person disappear.

Self help & reference